A Poster with Dragons

By Rolf A. F. Witzsche

Prologue

The four parts of this book are four chapters of my novel, Lu Mountain (chapter 10-13), presented singled out as a part of my Kaleidoscope project, because of their significance for understanding and healing the failures that gave rise to the greatest existential challenges in modern time, for individuals, nations, and the world.

Some of the challenges are the presently ongoing financial and economic collapse that has swept across the imperial West; the terror orgies, the fascist environmentalisms and depopulation policies; the extreme nuclear-war threats against Russia and China, with boasts that such a war is winnable; and not least the critically ignored start of the next Ice Age in the 2050s, if not sooner, in which the territories outside the tropics become uninhabitable, where presently most of humanity lives. In these arenas the power of love, humanity, scientific honesty, and spiritual development have fallen by the wayside.

This book is designed to focus on only one, and a rarely known aspect on the front of the failures, which is fundamental to the crisis. The aspect focused on in the book is the despotic nature of elitism, ranging from ecclesiastical and scientific despotism, all the way to political despotism.

The four parts presented here have been chosen for their progression on the theme of scientific freedom on which spiritual development depends that furnishes the foundation for civilization. More on the subject can be found in the Editorial at the end of the book.

My novel, Lu Mountain, from which the 4-part story is reproduced, is the last of the series of 12 novels named The Lodging for the Rose. The novel Lu Mountain is situated in China. The fictional story in the book begins in the wake of a cultural festival in a small fishing town on the great lake Poyang Hu. The protagonists live in a boat and had contributed to the festival by presenting the choral movement of Beethoven's 9th Symphony, played electronically from their boat. The main protagonists are a group of Americans living in exile in China, interfacing with a man named, Jacky, a high-level counterpart of a Chinese governmental institution.

Ecclesiastical despotism; denial of the fullness of God's creation; mortal man; a corporeal and sensual belief.

Contents

Part 1 - A Poster with Dragons

We were treated to a friendly dinner after the festival was concluded. At the dinner, we were presented a piece of Chinese art, a scene of Lu Mountain embroidered in silk. Jacky accepted the gift for us with a speech, in which he explained our mission in China.

After the official part of the welcome ceremony to the city was dispensed with, I asked Jacky to inquire with the head man if there might be an artist in the city who could create a Chinese style poster for me, personally.

"What kind of poster?" an older man asked from across the table. He spoke in broken English."

"A standard size poster with a three letter symbol inside a circle, surrounded by two dragons facing each other," I replied.

"I can do this for you, ' the man replied. He wore long gray hair and an almost as long, gray beard. "Come to my shop tomorrow and it will be done. Except, you have to tell me what the symbol is and what it means," he said, "so that I can create the right mood to match the symbol."

"The first part is easy." I said and bowed to the man as I thanked him for his kind offer. "The letters for the symbol are, CSD. Their meaning, however, is not that easily explained."

"I need to know, to be able to create the right mood," the artist repeated.

Since this was China and I lacked the means to explain in simple terms the scientific significance of the letters, the thought came to mind to create a story to convey the message. I told the man that, he being an artist would have the gift to determine the mood by listening to my story that presents in metaphor an extremely complex scientific issue.

He answered with a simple nod.

I told him that the story is about a king of a great kingdom. The king was honored throughout his realm and in many lands near and far. He was honored for his wisdom and for his ability to heal.

One day the sages came to the king and said, "teach us your wisdom, so that we can teach all the people in the kingdom." Being a kind person, the king agreed and set up a school in which he would teach the sages, in order that they could teach the people. The idea was a good one, but what could he teach them?

He thought about that question, then he decided that he would teach the sages certain principles that he had discovered, and how these principles can be applied to healing discords and diseases. He devised a course of instruction for them, and frequently, throughout the course he would tell his students to go out into the streets and prove the principles by healing someone, which they all did. In the end, after a full week of instruction and successful practicing had passed, he presented each of his students a certificate with the letters CSD placed thereon, drawn in an elaborate style of calligraphy.

"But what do the letters mean?" the students asked the king.

"The C stands for Christ," the king explained, "in honor of the world's most advanced Exemplar of the truth about God and man. The S stands for Science," the king added. "This letter symbolizes what I have taught you. It symbolizes, that what I have presented to you is not a philosophy which I have invented as philosophers do, but has been a presentation of discovered, verifiable, universal principles and their imperatives."

The king added that these principles and imperatives are far greater that he himself, and that he himself is but a student of the science involved in making these discoveries. He explained that in contrast to this, a philosophy is artificial and finite. He said that a philosophy is like a religious doctrine that is deemed absolute, whereby it closes the door to any form of a higher perception. The king explained that science is the opposite of that. It is not artificial, but is determined by the face of the universe, nor is it finite, as it always leaves the door open to a higher hypothesis to supersede what has been established at the leading edge of current perception.

"Science is the gateway to truth," the king added. "And the letter D stands for Doctor. It signifies to you that you have been taught by the best in the field, that you understand the nature of science and the principles that pertain to the leading edge of science. It also signifies that you have proven your understanding of it by applied healing. This means that you have all become full fledged scientists and deserve to be honored accordingly."

Thus, in honoring their achievement, the king allowed each one of the students to attach the letters CSD as a professional title to their name.

Eventually, the king became involved in other projects and therefore was forced to close the school. He simply couldn't spare the time for it. Still, his advisors prevailed on him, saying, "we need more teachers to teach the people." So again, being a kind and honorable man, the king considered their plea and consented.

Since he could no longer spare the time to teach himself, nor did he expect to live on this planet forever, he thought about what could be done to have the teaching continue without him. Soon, he found a solution. His solution was somewhat unique. He founded an academy that represented his wisdom and his discoveries of fundamental principles, and he established a provision that allowed every citizen of the realm to become a member of the academy as a kind of statement of recognition and acknowledgement of the king's principles. One this was done, he reopened the school as a part of the academy. This gave the teaching in the school a definition; a unique direction; a specific character.

Nevertheless, the king faced still one more dilemma, a threefold dilemma.

The first part of the dilemma was that he couldn't be certain that the school would actually provide bonafied scientific teaching, based on discovered, understood, and acknowledged, universal principles, in the manner as he had taught. Since he continued to be the school's president, he felt that it was his responsibility to assure that the school lived up to its billing.

His second dilemma was that he couldn't even be sure what would be taught. He could present a lesson plan, but he could never be sure that the teaching didn't come out as a statement of philosophy or religion, rather than as a platform of science that alone enables a person to engage in continuous self-development.

His third dilemma was that he couldn't just tell the future sages that, most likely, they would only be taught a philosophy in that school. Indeed, how would they be able to know the difference, not being able to understand the nature of science themselves, which they were hoping to be taught?

So the king sat down and puzzled about his dilemmas. He realized that he could solve some of his dilemmas by lowering the people's expectations, allowing the school to hand out only a bachelor degree with the symbols CSB. He felt that this would put the onus on the student's to upgrade themselves by means of their own scientific and spiritual development until in time they would be worthy of the king's degree of CSD; the doctor's degree.

9

Still, he had a problem with that. He had to ask himself: Who will determine when, in a person's self-development, the point is reached when philosophy is fully displaced by scientific perception? Who can make this determination for another except the scientist himself, or herself? Is anyone, except an experienced scientist able to separate science from philosophy, and know which of the two governs his heart? Not likely, right?

Since the king understood all of this, and being a scientist himself, he came up with a most elegant and elevating solution. He created two application forms for the royal academy. One form was designed for those citizens who have never been taught by a sage from the school. The second form he devised for the citizens who had been so taught, previously. Now the king inserted sample names into the forms, and the name that he chose for the counter-signer of the second form, was the name of a noted philosopher. In this manner the king pointed out to anyone who is able to see, to be aware that the teaching of the sages might really just be philosophy.

Of course, the king realized that this was only a part of the solution. He realized that he needed to find a way to make it possible for the citizens to determine for themselves when a teacher is a bonafied scientist, and not a philosopher.

So he puzzled some more about the problem. Then he reached a conclusion. He added a note to each of the application forms for academy membership, saying that the citizens must have the application countersigned either by a teacher who has received a degree, or by a teacher who has taken a degree.

The king was sure that this paradox would spark some thinking, because a philosopher would never recognize the legitimacy of a person simply taking a degree by his own volition, based on his deeply honest self-acknowledgement of having become a bonafied scientist; of having become a person who recognizes, understands, and acknowledges the nature of universal principles. The king realized that only a scientist who actually reaches this stage of development will feel impelled to 'take' or assume the degree that is associated with that achievement and attach it to his or her name as a title, according to the king's provision. With that, the king was satisfied.

"Did it work?" asked man.

I shook my head. "The degree that is taken in this manner will have to be the degree, CSD," I explained. "As I said, it is the kind of degree that only a scientist can take. In fact, it is the only degree that is not available to be given, since the king has stopped giving out that degree, and the academy itself could only give out a lesser degree."

"So, what's the point?" asked the man.

"The point is," I said, that the only degree that really matters, is the CSD degree that can only be taken, that can never be given. That gives the CSD symbol a profound meaning."

"But has anyone taken the CSD degree?" the man asked again.

I shook my head. I said I didn't know. I said that the onus for determining that answer was on the prospective student. "The king required the student to make this determination. It was for the student to determine who is qualified to countersign his application. That's a solemn responsibility," I said. I suggested to the man that our world would be secure if society would have heeded the king's directive. "Thus, the king said to himself: Every citizen will know from here on, which teacher is a scientist, and which is a philosopher."

"I wouldn't be surprised if no one took on the title, CSD," said the Chinese artist, "since such a step unfolds from a development that is not easily won. I think no one in the king's kingdom was ready for this."

I agreed. "Still, the king also knew that in due course, people would reach the stage at which the requisite realization is made. Then someone will take the degree CSD and people will recognize that this has indeed happened. They will recognize it by the good that comes out it. The king was content that this would happen even if he never saw the day of it in his own lifetime.

I explained to the artist across the table from me that the key element in this process of self-authorization is always one's honesty with oneself, especially one's scientific honesty about the imperatives of universal principles. I suggested to the artist that the CSB stage is a precarious stage, the kind of stage at which a person will likely see something of the scientific dimension, but where that person is vulnerable of regressing into becoming a philosopher. On the other hand, it is also a stage where a person becomes fascinated with the infinite potential of science and therefore engages in his or her scientific and spiritual self-development.

I explained to the artist that the CSD symbol on the poster that I was looking for, has four meanings: It symbolizes a title of achievement that no one can bestow or withhold, except one's own honesty with oneself. To a citizen who walks with open eyes, such a title would inspire trust in the teacher. To the academy itself, it is a title that the academy is no longer responsible for. The academy is responsible only for what it bestows, or can bestow, or withhold. In real terms, the CSD title is a symbol that assures humanity's infinite self-development. No scientific development can occur, nor will occur, outside of the parameters that the CSD symbol represents. "It is therefore the only degree in the world that represents infinite development, a movement at the leading edge."

"Can you create such a poster?" I asked the artist.

The man nodded. "But what about the dragons?" the artist added. "What characteristics shall I give them? What do they represent?"

"They represent the warfare between science and philosophy," I answered. "If the world is dark, the dragons are ferocious beasts and will fight to destroy humanity. But in the sunshine they cannot fight. They become a benign power, so I have been told. This means that the CSD symbol represents humanity's light, the sunshine of its Soul."

I explained to the artist that a philosopher would never acknowledge the CSD degree that a scientist takes, based on his honesty with himself. A philosopher is someone who always seeks external authorization, like Hobbes and all the other war philosophers of the 16th Centuries who were richly paid for their philosophies that authorized the unrestrained rule of their king. A philosopher is conditioned by the system of philosophy to acknowledge only an externally sanctioned authority, an authority that he lacks, since a philosophy is merely opinion without an anchor in scientific understanding that would authorize a demonstrable perception to be regarded as truth no matter what anybody says. A philosopher seeks his authorization from another person since he lacks the authority of science. In this conflict over authority, especially the authority that shapes public opinion, the philosopher will wage war against the scientist, as he must do, in order to be true to himself as a philosopher who acknowledges no such thing as a truth. Except, the philosopher will not win this war. I told the artist that this outcome was understood in 1648, and also much earlier in very ancient times. I told him that there exist a very old tale of a contest between science and philosophy.

The tale takes place in Egypt. The scientist is Moses. Facing the might and arrogance of the Pharaoh of Egypt, Moses asks his student to throw his staff onto the ground before Pharaoh. The staff promptly becomes transformed into a serpent. In response, Pharaoh commands all his philosophers, magicians, wizards, and elite to do the same. As they do, indeed, their staffs likewise became transformed into serpents. But Moses' student's serpent ate up their serpents. Every one of them. Thus the contest ended. Moses then asked his student to pick up his serpent by the tail, which thereby became a staff again.

12

"In this manner the contest will end for mankind, between science and philosophy, religion, magic, wizardry, and elitism of any sort," I said to the artist. "But this time is not here yet. We still live in a world in which the two dragons face each other in that contest that philosophy, religion, and elitism cannot win."

"And the circle?" the artist asked. "What is its significance."

"The circle protects the degree, CSD," I replied.

I explained that a circle has no beginning and no end. As such it reflects the nature of universal principles that science explores and makes accessible to us, which likewise have neither beginning nor end. They simply existed before time was and will always remain the same. Nor can a circle ever be mathematically described with absolute accuracy, just like reality can never be absolutely described in science, or else the infinite would become finite and development would end, and all would become philosophy.

"Now my friend," I said to the artist, "can you create a poster that represents all of these aspects?"

The man nodded. "Come to my shop tomorrow and it will be ready for you. Nor will I charge you for it. I will create the poster and retain the copyright, and then produce ten more."

"Why just ten more?" I asked. "Why not produce ten million more, and publish the story that stands behind it, and uplift the people of China with it, and the whole world? Why shouldn't the truth about human development also pave the way to commercial success when it begins to uplift people's life?"

"Give me the copyright to the story and that may happen," the man replied and began to smile.

As I reached my hand across the table for a handshake, I said to him, "My friend, you have it, as Jacky is your witness."

Jacky nodded and grinned.

Afterwards, as we were about to leave, I took the artist aside. He introduced himself as Lee. I told him about the development in our own family that led up to the CSD symbol. I told him our coffee, sex, and biscuit story, out of which the CSB symbol developed, which became from its very inception synonymous with total honesty with oneself and with one another, including a scientific honesty to the imperatives of universal principles. I told him how the meaning of the symbolism became uplifted later on in the flow of our continuously ongoing scientific development, until all the philosophical elements related to sex, marriage, and so forth, became completely supplanted with the scientific recognition of universal principles, and an understanding of these principles, and our full acknowledgement of them. I explained to him that once that point is reached, the CSB symbol becomes superseded, just as philosophical concepts become superseded with scientific recognition. "Thus, the CSD symbol takes its place and becomes symbolic as a new mile stone for a new and brighter world with its new dimension."

Lee indicated that he understood now why this poster, with its story attached, could be valuable to the whole of humanity as a way-marker on the horizon of its own scientific development.

Part 2 - Flood Tides of Love

As we left the restaurant where the city had hosted its welcoming dinner for us, a young woman approached us from behind. She thanked us for coming to her city. She told us that she was impressed by my analysis of what drives scientific development. She also told us proudly that she is the head instructor of the local college, a kind of University College, as she described it. She wondered if we would like to make a formal presentation along the same lines that we had talked about, but to the whole college.

Jacky looked at Steve and grinned. Steve looked at me. "How about it, Doctor?" he said and began to laugh.

"Tomorrow at two," I replied to the woman. "Before that, please join us on the ship for lunch. Oh yes, I also need you to supply some educational materials. I need two water glasses, empty. Four empty bottles, and for bottles filled with fruit juice or colored water."

The woman looked puzzled, but agreed.

She was precisely on time. At twelve o'clock sharp she stood at our door on the Lu Rose. Wai-ye received her. She showed her around on the ship. Lunch was already set up on the upper deck; two kinds of rice, vegetables, fried fish, pastry from the market. It wasn't a fancy lunch, but the atmosphere made up for it. To be honored by this woman as our guest, somehow made the occasion special.

"What do you need the bottles for?" she asked during lunch.

"Knowing Peter," said Tony, "he will use these bottles to teach your students a lesson they will not forget for their entire life." He began to laugh.

She looked at me with a questioning look.

"You will see," I replied, "just trust me. Also, rest assured, what I present won't be hard to understand, but it will be profoundly significant to the students." Then I grinned. Moments later she joined in until we all began to laugh.

At the school, it was I who was surprised. It seemed as if the entire school was assembled in the auditorium. There was standing room only, and even some of that was taken up.

I told the students that would speak to them in very broad terms to illustrate certain principles. I warned them that the real world isn't as clearly delineated. Then I began.

"What is a human being?" I asked. "What sets us apart from every other living species on this planet? What is it that makes us human?"

Wai-ye translated the questions.

I told them the answer myself. I told them that our humanity lies in our ability to think and to understand complex phenomena by understanding the principles that govern them. We discern patterns of reality, discover principles, create hypotheses about a certain phenomenon, we test the hypotheses, we refine them, we test them again, and so we derive at an understanding of truth, of verifiable truth. The process is called scientific discovery. Then we build on this discovered truth. We create a culture for ourselves that is supported with industries and technologies that are all built on our scientific understanding of the truths that we have discovered. With these, we support our existence. Herein lies the proof of the truth. The truth becomes manifest in the state of our civilization. What enables out civilization to grow and become more secure and more beautiful, is an element of Truth. The process that makes all of this happen, that enables us to do all this, and to carry it forward, is called humanist education.

I took a glass from the table and held it up. I told them that it is the task of humanist education to fill our individual glass to the very brim with all the aspects that we need in our life. That process set our existence apart from that of an animal.

"So, let's see what we need to put in there," I said.

I told them that we need to fill these glasses with the products of our scientific development. I told then that this development has certain spiritual aspects, certain physical and technological aspects, certain cultural aspects, and certain sociological aspects, each of which has a unique type of science associated with it.

"Now I am going to tell you what I mean with that," I said to them.

16

I explained that a human being is a sentient being. This means that we have the capacity to be aware of ourselves, of who we are as the tallest species of life in the universe as far as we know it. Then, as we utilize this human capacity do discover, to see with the mind's eye what the physical eye cannot behold, we gain a realization, an understating of our world, and treasure that understanding because we can enrich our world with the products of that understanding. In this way we find great treasures imbedded in our humanity. We also find that the recognition of these treasures in our humanity inspire us to treat one another with the honor and dignity that our wondrous humanity is worth, which is very precious. Thus, we recognize love as a fundamental principle that unfolds out of our self-respect as human beings, and our respect for one another and for what we are as human beings. We also recognize this discovered principle to be a universal principle, because we all share the same humanity; the same beautiful Soul, as it were; the same intelligence; the same creativity, and so on. Thus, we recognize the principle of universal love as a fundamental, universal principle of civilization. We acknowledge this principle in countless different ways as we enrich one another and enrich our world with it. We find the truth of our humanity reflected in creations of beauty, music, art, literature, poetry, technology, science, and so on. Thus, we also recognize in this principle of universal love that we are all married to one another by the single humanity that we all share.

This knowledge of our universal marriage, or universal love, creates a mutually supportive civilization, a civilization that we feel honored to enrich with the fruits of our labor and our intellect. In this manner we build this civilization; a human civilization; and stand up for it and protect it, and fight for it if need be. We are even prepared to fight for our humanity when there is little hope that we will see the rewards for it in our lifetime. Still we are committed to do what must be done to assure the survival of our civilization as a worthwhile testament to the fact that we have lived as a human being on this planet.

Having said this, I picked up the empty glass again and the bottle that I had labeled, the science of universal marriage, and filled the empty glass a quarter full.

I explained further, that as human beings we also have a variety of physical needs. We need food, clothing, shelter, water, energy, transportation, household goods, educational materials, cultural materials, health care, and so on. And we need industries to produce these goods, and infrastructures for the industries. Also, we need a financial system that furnishes an equitable interface between the individual needs of people, and their labor to fulfill these needs. We call the whole structure with every part working together, an economy.

I suggested to the students that they might find it interesting to search for the underlying principles of that economy. I suggested that they should ask themselves where society's wealth is located. Is it located in money? Is it located in property? Or is it located in its productive industries that fulfill its needs, and in the human ingenuity and labor that operates these industries? Evidently, money is the least contributing element, and therefore the least valuable element of the whole equation, being nothing more than just a regulatory tool. By the same token, the human element becomes the most essential, and therefore the most valuable element.

I suggested that if this underlying principle is understood, an economy functions well, because the focus will them be placed on what matters most, the development of the human intellect, such as society's scientific and technological development, the development of its skills, its health, and the development of efficient energy sources and processes that increase the effectiveness of human labor.

Having said this, I picked up the glass again and the bottle that I labeled the Science of Physiology, or physical economy, and filled the glass to the half-full mark.

I pointed out that there is another major area in which the human being stands miles apart from the animal world, and that's the domain of dialog. Animals are able to communicate with one another in a primitive sense, but only human beings are capable of linguistic dialog. We have developed languages, complex languages that give us the capacity to share our discoveries and to preserve them for future ages by which we individually, gain a certain immortality. Except this is only the smallest part of the linguistic dialog. We are also constantly in communication with ourselves. We call this thinking. When we face a paradox, we use our spoken language to evaluate the evidence. We speak to ourselves in our thoughts, as we search to discover the underlying principles. For this we need a language. A high-level language. In this communication with ourselves we begin to discern complex universal truths. We begin to resolve paradoxes. Without a complex language, our thoughts will be fettered. They will be limited to primitive perceptions. At this primitive level our dialogs become useless chattering and accomplish nothing. That is why Homer, for instance, who practically created the Greek language in 500 BC, with his epic poetry, is being recognized as the foundation for the Greek Classical Period that became one of the greatest periods of scientific achievement in human history. In like manner did Dante lay the foundation for the Golden Renaissance.

With this said, I filled the cup up some more. I filled it three quarters full, from the bottle labeled the Science of Dialog.

"But there is still more to a human being than this," I said. I explained that the human being is an infinite being with a capacity to develop further and further. It is in that, where we find our riches; not in money, but in ourselves; in our capacity to develop ourselves, and with it our world. In order to achieve this, we require a certain commitment to ourselves, individually, and on the universal platform as a nation and the world. We need to make this commitment on the platform of committing ourselves to certain understood and acknowledged fundamental principles, which are universal principles. I told them that we call the declaration of these principles, a constitution. Obviously, this has to be done with a scientific approach. It can't be done arbitrarily. The constitution has to reflect verifiable truth; universal principles that have proven their worth in the advance of civilization. The U.S. Federal Constitution is an example of this type, which sets up a foundation for the general welfare; common defense; freedom to develop; the pursuit of happiness. All of these have been recognized to greatly enrich human society as a whole.

Another great constitution that was created, is the Treaty of Westphalia. This constitution contains the declared understanding and acknowledgement of the principle of universal love. It is an international constitution that was established as a platform that brought to an end eighty years of devastating wars.

Still another great constitution, further back in time, is the platform of a recognition of certain humanist principles and truths that became the foundation for the Golden Renaissance. These recognized and understood truths literally established the image of man in the image of God.

With this said, I filled the glass to the brim from the bottle labeled: The Science of the Constitution.

"But humanity is presently at war," I said, changing the tone. I pointed out that the imperial oligarchy of the world, the fundi, have launched an unending war against humanity to eradicate all the human elements that threaten their feudal empire. The fundi have done this after the Renaissance powers nearly eliminated their key empire, the empire of Venice. In a sense, this process of destruction of any movement towards a new renaissance is still continuing. The ruling empire of today sees itself as having to do this in order to save its existence. A highly developed society will never allow itself to become slaves or

19

to act as slaves in the service of an imperial oligarchy; or allow itself to be looted; nor allow anyone else to be looted. This built in humanist resolve was well demonstrated in 1510 when the League of Cambria was formed by the Renaissance powers with one single goal, to rid the world of the looting empire of Venice. It was a noble movement. It should have worked. It didn't. The Pope prevented it. Nevertheless, the humanist idea continued on. It raised its head many times in history, even though it was beaten back repeatedly by the imperial forces.

The strength of a people's resolve to free humanity from domination was well demonstrated to Winston Churchill of the British Empire, by President Franklin Delanor Roosevelt. Roosevelt made it clear that a commitment to defend human freedom would always be found whenever a highly developed Renaissance exists in society, of the type that he had helped to establish in the USA, that had touched the whole world and won its fight against fascism. Out of the resources of the Franklin Roosevelt inspired renaissance the USA had become the largest and literally the only globally significant economic and military power on the planet. Roosevelt announced at this point that the British Empire would have to be dismantled. He pointed out to Churchill that the society of humanity won't stand for colonialism any longer, that colonialism was doomed by the unfolding humanist environment. Unfortunately, Roosevelt died at this point. With that, the fight for humanity came to a halt once more. In fact, it was reversed. The imperials won again. But how did they do it?

None of the students was aware of how this had been done, how the greatest humanist development of the 20th Century was defeated.

It was done quietly, in the background. It was done through the baby boom generation. A large new generation was born. But would they be allowed to be educated as human beings? The very thought must have scared the imperial oligarchy to death. The entire imperial structure would be doomed if a vast new generation would be brought up on the platform of a powerful humanist renaissance like the one that Franklin Roosevelt had pioneered, who had threatened the empire in no uncertain terms. The thought of seeing a new generation growing up on this platform must have frightened the imperial oligarchy even more than it had been frightened in 1508 with its existence was threatened by the Renaissance powers. Thus, an effort was launched, especially in America, through the back door, to destroy this threat of a new renaissance at its very root.

And how was this done?

I didn't even wait for an answer. It was done by depriving the coming generation of the substance of its humanity, its education; thereby creating a generation of 'empty' people.

Towards this end the oligarchy, the fundi, dredged up from their mud pool all the counter-humanist philosophies and ideologies that they had established over the ages for similar purposes. Then they took the mud-grown stuff and gradually flooded the nations' education systems with it. The mud products consisted of irrational ideologies; ideologies without principle; ideologies that look fancy, but are hollow shells; empty structures that don't produce anything in terms of elevating society while they take up space in consciousness. These ideologies and philosophies are of a type that can be likened to the Emperor's New Clothes of Hans Christian Anderson's fairy tale. Everyone exclaimed over the beauty of the new clothes that Emperor wore, while in reality there was nothing there. It was said that these clothes could only be seen by someone intelligent enough to see them. Thus, the people all lied to themselves, and the Emperor who walked around naked was hailed.

I suggested to the students, that if one takes anyone of these mud-grown philosophies and ideologies, that suddenly everyone was induced to believe in, and adds up everything they have ever accomplished for the good of humanity, the combined total would amount to zero.

"So, let me illustrate how this process works that creates empty people," I added.

I took the bottle labeled "Adam Smith." I shook it well, and proceeded to pour from it into an empty glass, liberally. Then I took the glass and turned it upside down to illustrate that it is still empty, since nothing came out of it.

I told the students that Adam Smith says that greed makes the world go round; that the whole society benefits by an individual's greed. That's a lie. No principle supports that. Nor does the reality support that, as it is illustrated by the most far reaching social experiment in modern history, which in the USA was a generation dedicated to Adam Smith that accomplished nothing. Nevertheless, what Adam Smith says make a lot of sense to a hollow person that has been deprived of developing its humanity. After all, to a default person that lives like an animal, steeped in greed because that person knows nothing else, greed is the only thing that he's got left to live by as the animals do. Adam Smith creates and caters to such a person's mentality. Naturally, Adam's greed based economics is totally embraced by such a person, because Adam says what this person wants to hear. Thus, Adam Smith becomes celebrated as a great genius, or some kind of a god while society slowly dies from within.

I took the empty cup again and asked why the cup is empty. I said the reason is that Adam Smith is a liar, because there is no verifiable truth in what he says. I pointed out that America's baby boomers had used Adam Smith for thirty-five years, and their children have used him, and what was accomplished? They have taken the richest and most powerful economy on the planet and reduced it to nothing more than an empty shell, and half the world along with it. America's industries are largely gone; destroyed by free trade and other types of looting. The world-financial system is another casualty, an empty shell. The once healthy system of a Renaissance based economy became destroyed by a vast competition throughout the world in stealing from one another. The western population, the Adam Smith population, is now totally 'hollow' to the point that it can no longer produce the things that are necessary to sustain its existence. America lives of the labors of other nations, like Rome one did. It is literally unqualified for anything more than to exist as a consumer society. For that reason, it has been enslaving the world like the Roman Empire had enslaved everyone that was in reach of its long arms. The Roman society too, didn't know anymore how to produce what it needed, and had no inclination to learn to do so. It simply died with a whimper on its lips.

"Indeed, why would the baby boomers want to produce anything? Have they not been educated by Hobbes?" I asked.

I took the bottle labeled "Hobbes" and poured out liberally into the empty glass. And again, as I turned the glass upside down, there was nothing in it. "Why is this so?" I asked.

I answered that Thomas Hobbes has no principle to support his babbling. He speaks empty words. He says that love has no place in the world, except maybe in the smallest domain, in the privacy between two people. His motto is that human beings are animals, and in the animal world, "might is right," he said. He says that a person has every right to steal what others cannot defend. Thus society destroys one another and calls this a process of bettering itself. Evidently, this can't work. There is no chance that it can work. It is an empty dream that it will work. The reality is, that Hobbes was one of the war philosophers that dragged the nations of Europe into the hell hole of eighty years of war that degenerated into the worst military escapade in history, prior to World War Two. Still, Hobbes is celebrated as a hero today. Why?

The reason is simple. Hobbes says to society that human beings are animals, therefore we should recognize ourselves that way and act accordingly. I pointed out that this kind of talk makes a lot of sense to a generation that is being prevented from developing itself into effective human beings. Hobbes, therefore, makes sense to a hollow generation that lives on the level of animals; a generation of fascist animals that supports destruction, the use of force, the rage of killing people. In a very real sense, this deprived, default society, has become cultivated to become fascist killers. To such people, the song, "Might equals Right," is indeed a sweet song, which is being sung again with fanfares and speeches about our heroic readiness to use nuclear weapons in pre-emptive adventures to wipe other nations off the map. We may not be quite there yet, but we are singing that type of song already and evermore loudly.

I suggested to the students that it doesn't take a great scientist to figure out that this approach doesn't build a civilization. If one adds up Hobbes and all the others like him, the end result is still zero. That's why the glass remains empty.

After this, I took the bottle labeled "the empiricists and the romanticists," and poured out from the bottle into the still empty glass, liberally. And again, the glass remained empty. Why?

I suggested that the reason in this case, for the glass being empty, is that these zero-sum philosophies are all hollow in themselves. The philosophers themselves admit this, and are proud of it. They say there is no such thing as truth, all is opinion. No dialogs please! Don't talk to me about truth, you violate my opinion, I don't want to hear of it! If you face a paradox, don't puzzle over it. Life is full of paradoxes. Besides, you are an animal, you're not supposed to think. The very best you can do in this case, is to form an opinion, and to help you, I will tell you what your opinion ought to be. I give you the information. It is save for you to accept that, because it is after all, only an opinion. The key is harmony. Get along with other people's opinions. Don't fight for such abstract ideas as truth!

Naturally, to a person who is hollow inside, the words "don't think!" sound like music. Thus, two entire generations have been brought up on this 'music,' without an ability to think. The end result is that the world has been thrown into a frenzy of worshiping opinions, like the opinion that Ariel Sharon is a man of peace, which is about as far removed from the truth as is the moon from the earth. In fact, he would feel insulted to be called a man of peace.

An empty generation loves this kind of stuff, because it allows it to say anything it likes, since there is no requirement to prove anything, or support anything with a verifiable hypothesis. Thus, they cry: Deregulate the economy!

Let everyone's opinion prevail. Don't talk about truth. Don't talk about physical reality. Talk about freedom in accounting practices.

I suggested to the students that the empiricists' and the romanticists' bottle is empty, because there is nothing in it that adds anything of substance to the maintenance and advance of civilization.

Next, I took the bottle that I had labeled "The Roman Pantheon," and poured from it liberally into the empty glass, and turned the glass upside down to illustrate that it remained empty. "Why did it remain empty?" I asked again.

I explained that a Pantheon results, when there is no constitution governing society. The Roman Emperor might have explained: Well, isn't every animal in the field entitled to live like an animal to its own liking? Sadly, this is still being said today about the human society. We have created two generations of people who have chosen the model of the Pantheon for their constitution, and rightfully so, because they lack the background to see themselves as human beings of a common humanity.

They say, if I want to shoot dope, I should have the right to do so, and if I want to sell dope to make a buck, I should have the right to do that too. And the energy pirate says: If I have a chance to fleece society with outrageous electricity rates, I should have the right to do that also. And the Israeli leader says, if I want to bulldoze a few Palestinian homes to the ground, I should have the right to do that, and kill the inhabitants if I want. And then the President comes along and says, well you guys, if I feel afraid of another country I should have the right to wipe out the whole nation. Finally, the police chief taps you on the shoulder and says to you, well my son, since I don't like the way you look at me, I'll throw you in the brink for the rest of your life, because I have just claimed for myself the right to do that.

I suggested that the pantheonic development leads to ever-greater insanity, which obviously doesn't contribute anything to the advance of a civilization. Therefore, the glass remains empty.

I explained to the students that these zero-sum philosophies and ideologies aren't actually dangerous to anyone. I pointed out that they really don't have any power in themselves. I suggested that none of them could ever defeat someone like Plato or Leibnitz, for instance. I pointed out that their destructive effect has quite a different cause; namely, that they take up space, or more correctly, they demand us to give them space in our consciousness by throwing away valuable elements of our humanity that should be there, that should never be denied.

24

I illustrated to the students what this means.

I took a pitcher that holds three cups of liquid and filled it to the brim with fruit juice. I equated the contents in the pitcher with the contents of our humanity, such as; our love, integrity, generosity, sovereignty; also our intellect, our productive capacity, our universal good; as well as our capacity for making discoveries and for spiritual understanding; all the substance of ourselves as human beings that we require to create a civilization.

That's what a full pitcher looks like," I said to the students. "But then along come the synarchists, and they say to you: What you've got in your pitcher is nothing compared to what we can give you. So each one of them comes along and says to you: Pour out from what you have in there, pour out just one cup of it and throw it away, and let me fill this void with what is really good for you."

I mimicked Adam Smith saying: "There exists no principle of universal good. So, my son, throw that notion away. Greed is where the wealth of society is anchored."

With having said this, I poured out a single cup of juice from the pitcher and poured it down the sink.

Then I mimicked Thomas Hobbes saying: "There is no such thing as universal love in real life. My son, throw that notion away. All men are evil. Your welfare rests with the rule of might."

With having said this, I poured out another cup of juice from the pitcher and poured it down the sink.

Then I mimicked the empiricists and romanticists saying: "Forget the very notion of Truth, my son. Throw it away! There is no such thing as knowable truth. Give up wasting your time with that and be happy by devoting your life to whatever makes you feel good."

With having said this, I poured now a third cup of juice from the pitcher and poured it down the sink. Actually it was just colored water that poured away, but the empiricists believed me. Then I held the pitcher up high and turned it upside down so that everybody could see that it was now empty. It was empty because I poured everything way that was in there, and never added anything back.

Having illustrated beyond a shadow of a doubt that the pitcher was now empty, I simply repeated what I had illustrated before. I poured liberally from the bottle labeled "Adam Smith," into a cup, and poured the contents from the cup into the pitcher; and likewise from the bottle labeled "Thomas Hobbes" and from the bottle labeled the "empiricists and the romanticists," and so forth.

Having done all this, I held the pitcher up high once again and turned it upside down, to illustrate that it was still empty.

"What makes this illustration different from the first illustration?" I asked the students.

Since no one spoke up, I answered the question myself. "The difference is in the way we regard education," I said. "With the first illustration, I proved to you that the synarchists have nothing to offer. Every time I filled a cup, there was nothing there. In other words, any young person who is educated by this system receives no education at all, even after having been spoon fed on these zero sum philosophies for all their academic years."

I laughed. "As you have seen," I said, "the entire contents of three empty cups poured out into the pitcher added up to nothing, right?"

I paused and added in a serious tone that this zero-sum effect actually creates only half of the problem. "That's why the second illustration is needed," I said, "because it points to where the real danger lies. The real danger is, that the synarchists take away everything that is vital of humanity."

I pointed away what I started with in the second illustration. I started with a full pitcher, but ended up with an empty one. "In real life, this means, that a young person starts out with a full and rich humanity, and ends up with every aspect of that humanity totally denied."

I pointed out to the students that every human being starts with a full pitcher. I said, "It is not the role of education to fill this pitcher to the brim. Each human being has its pitcher already full. This means that the real role of education is to make us more fully aware of our humanity and its riches, and of the universal principles that it represents. The synarchists take all of this away, and have intensely done this for decades. They have literally robbed the people of their humanity. They have placed their humanity so far out of reach, by means of crafty lies, that their 'education' actually left them empty inside. They have dragged society down to the level of animals, and lower than that; to the level of beasts, of fascist beasts; to a kind of default state from where one simply can't sink any lower. If you take away everything that is human, there is nothing left that sets a person apart from an animal. And that is where the danger lies for society."

Here I had to laugh again. "The irony is that the synarchists are not dangerous in themselves," I said. "They have no real power. The danger is in that we given them the power they seek, when we respond to their bidding. That is why I call them synarchists. They are cynical, and they get everybody to run against everybody else in an well-orchestrated synchronized manner. That's what the Adam Smith synarchism does. It says to everybody, 'greed is good; be greedy and steal from everybody you can steal from.' And that is what everybody did. The financial 'market' became an arena in which everybody is pitted against everybody else. The divine Principle of universal good went out the window, completely, and with it the prosperity of society went out of the window. When Franklin Roosevelt died in 1945, America was the richest nation on the planet, with an economy so powerful that it could have revolutionized the world. Instead of utilizing that wealth for the good of humanity, the American people were intensively educated to become 'empty' people. In that process of becoming 'empty' people, America destroyed most of its industries, threw its skilled workforce onto the trash heap, and became the biggest debtor in the world. Before the whole thing disintegrated, America had amassed forty thousand billions of dollars in debt. That is how the Adam Smith synarchists set everybody against everybody else, in order to eradicate the slightest awareness in society of the principle of universal good, the principles of its humanity."

I pointed out that the Thomas Hobbes type synarchists did the same thing socially, by eradicating the very notion that love is a universal principle that needs to be manifest universally. I pointed out that the eradication of the principle of universal love opened the gates to the Thirty Years War, and to every war thereafter.

I further pointed out that the romanticist synarchists eradicated the very notion of universal Truth in the same manner, saying, "There is no truth in anything, there is not even any truth in such a thing as a humanity. We are all animals. It's all opinion."

I pointed out that with the very notion of Truth banned, the self-denial of society became so deep that nobody had any moral strength left to stand in the way of the imperials' goals; not in Roman times, nor in our time. "Our world has become more fascist than Rome had ever been," I concluded. "Who even thinks about the principle of universal good anymore in today's world, and acts with generosity, or even universal love? The synarchists have enlisted society into their ranks, even to spit in the face of God, as it were, and we in America hail ourselves of having become the foremost champions in that pursuit.

I pointed out to the students that it is totally possible to disable an entire generation of people with this deeply disabling kind of education, even two successive generations in a row. I told them that in my own country a third generation of young people is now being disabled in the same manner. I suggested to the students, that in order for them to understand what all of this means in real life terms, we would now need to look at what such an 'emptied' person looks like, who has been deprived of everything that manifests our humanity.

I pointed out that a human being is always a human being, whether that person is educated or not. In other words, the potential is always there to develop that humanity that we all share. I compared the human potential to a racing car, which is of no use to anyone if one doesn't know how to start the engine. For a human being to become effective in a modern society a certain level of humanist education is required to get the engine going. "In other words, we have to discover the value of the principle of universal good, which is the key element of our humanity, so that we won't be tempted to privatize everything that is good, and thereby deny its character and loose it altogether. If one doesn't have that kind of education that brings out our generosity, our integrity, our industry and intellect, and so forth; nothing good happens in the real world, and everything good that has been established, will fall apart.

"Except, where does this leave us, living in a world that is ruled by a hollow generation?" I asked. "Don't we then end up living in a hollowed out world that threatens to collapse into nothing?"

I suggested that the answer be, Yes. I also suggested that this answer must be followed up with another question, namely: What must we do to be able to survive in this disintegrating world? "The answer is simple," I said. "If our glass is empty, then let's put something in it that has substance. Let's pour into it the substance of our humanity in flood tides of universal love. All the stuff that we poured into our glass before were flood tides of voids. That's why the glass remained empty and nothing ever came out of it. Empire is that kind of default state. It unfolds when the flow of universal love isn't happening. It is a void like darkness is a void of light, and so is everything that is a part of this darkness, of the void called empire and reflects this void, such as empiricism, imperialism, and the insanity of romanticism as related to Rome, or the modern versions of these in the form of Hobbesian fascism and Adam Smith's fascism of greed. They are all voids of substance, the absence of the substance of love. When nothing comes out of our glass, and consequently nothing productively happens on the human scene, so that civilization disintegrates, then we have only one option before us. We have to pour something of substance into our glass. We have to pour into our world flood tides of love to fill the void, and that means flood tides of universal love for our humanity, love for what we are and are constructively capable of as human beings. It means universal love in terms of discovering of the boundless dimension of the human mind in creativity, reason, the recognition of the principles of the universe, scientific understanding, efficient living, creating technologies, infrastructures, culture, music, literature, art, beauty, and so on. Universal love flows from all of these aspects that makes us truly human. Universal love is rooted in truth, and manifest itself as honor, integrity, gentleness, caring, but also as joy and passion for living a human life. None of these are found in the void, in the emptiness of empire, in the darkness of greed, in the sewer of empiricism, destruction, war, and hate. So, it is important to learn to love universally, to embrace our humanity, to enrich it, and to heal whatever needs healing. Without pouring flood tides of love into the human scene we won't develop a rich civilization, and the civilization that we have will disintegrate. Our world will become empty, as I have illustrated with the empty glass when nothing of substance is poured into it, because the glass stands in metaphor for out world."

I pointed out to the student's surprise that the answer to that question of universal love has already been put forward long before the question was even asked by anyone. I pointed out that the answer has been put forward in modern times by a man who understood the answer already thirty-five years ago; who has been in a battle to get people to look at themselves and take the necessary steps to refill their individual glasses to the brim. The man's battle has been a battle for scientific, spiritual, and technological development, to create a real economy, and to cause the same to happen throughout the world. He spoke about humanist development; universal principles; scientific dialogs of the highest order and on the whole front, including a dialog of cultures to unite the world. He also spoke about the constitutional principles, the sovereignty of nations, and the principle of universal love. He also talked for many years about a new constitution for humanity, a new financial constitution, a new Bretton Woods type world-financial system based on fixed exchange rates, built on proven universal principles.

I suggested to the students that this man evidently knows the four bottles that represent the four essential domains of science which develop the substance of humanity, and he pours from them liberally.

I asked them to look at what it is that he pours from the bottle of the science of universal marriage. I suggested that his hope is for a world of perfectly sovereign nation states existing in a community of principle, rather than an imperial world ruled by force, terror, and the arrogance of might. "He sees the people of the world as one humanity, and that perceived universally of our humanity, reflecting the principle if universal good, is reflected in all of his efforts."

I pointed out that the evidence is founded in his large scale physical development proposals for Europe, North America, Africa, all of Eurasia, South America, the Middle East; development proposals on a huge scale that offer humanity a chance to live again. He speaks about infrastructure development in terms of a universal love for people that knows no boundaries or borders; which always, in the end, means universal human development as a means for enriching one another and to enrich our world as a whole. And he goes on fighting this battle today, against a hollowed out society living in a hollowed out world.

I pointed out that he also knows the second bottle well, and pours from it freely, the bottle of the science of physiology. He also understands the principle of economy as having both a human and a physical dimension. The first is a dimension of technologies and the infrastructures created by the human mind, while the physical dimension represents the products created on that platform. Where the zero-sum philosopher says, money is wealth, that man says, money is merely a tool. He says that society's wealth is in the human genius, which needs to be developed to its fullest potential. He says that only a sovereign, national, federal bank, that doesn't exist for profit, can operate on the acknowledged platform that money is not wealth, but a tool to develop the real wealth of mankind that is located in the human genius.

I pointed out that this man also knows the third bottle with the label, the Science of Dialog. No scientific, political, or economic leader has raised the language of dialog to a higher level in modern history, than did this man. He is known and honored throughout the world for his extraordinary speeches, articles, and in-depth scientific papers, which he has put out, and still does, with a speed that is bewildering. The speed is consistently such, that if one thinks one understands the man, finally, one always finds that he has moved two more steps ahead again.

I further pointed out that this man also knows the fourth bottle well, labeled the Science of the Constitution. He honors that science as no one else does. He speaks about the U.S. Federal Constitution in scientific terms, especially its Preamble, as a foundation for the nation, and he goes beyond it. He proposes the adoption of a global constitution that includes three elements. The first element involves the world's rededication to the principle of universal love, along the line of the 1648 Treaty of Westphalia, which was the word's first major global constitution, and the greatest ever devised. His constitutional proposal is to use this platform and put the currently bankrupt world-financial system through a bankruptcy reorganization, in order to save the world economy from disintegrating totally. This constitutional principle worked in the past; it ended eighty years of war that had wiped out half the population of Europe. It has the potential to work again to save humanity from a worse fate.

The second element of his world constitutional proposal is for the nations to recommit themselves to a new Bretton Woods type, world-financial system, with fixed exchange rates as a minimal standard for global economic recovery and industrial development. He sees this constitutional proposal as a replacement for the presently ruling Pantheon of floating exchange rate speculation.

His third constitutional element for the world, is for humanity as a whole to commit itself to the building of the Eurasian Land Bridge and its global extension, as a minimal commitment to achieve a workable global economic development, including the extremely urgent redevelopment of Africa that has become a dying continent, as have many other places. One natural aspect of this global constitutional commitment will be the elimination of slave labor sweat shops, and an end to the enslavement of children that has currently trapped over two-hundred-fifty million children into a state of developmental hopelessness.

Finally, I told the students that this man who did all these things and is still doing them, who has presented the only possible answer to the current crisis and has done so for thirty-five years, is none other than the renowned American economist, scientist, and statesman, the eight times declared candidate for the U.S. Presidency, Lyndon H. LaRouche; the one man that is most feared by the imperial oligarchy and the most slandered by them, especially in America. The man is greatly honored everywhere else, and may be the most sought after political, economic, and pedagogical advisor in the world.

I suggested to the students that the battle lines for the future are clearly drawn. One finds on one side a hollow generation of people who have lost their humanity, and literally their ability to survive; who have become fascists armed with nuclear bombs; and on the other one finds the hated and slandered Lyndon LaRouche proposing infrastructures for survival that humanity has been coerced to reject. Indeed, a hallow generation of people does find it very hard to look above its default state of an animal type fascist existence and find the substance for its survival in the higher dimension of its humanity that it has been denied to experience for its entire life.

I pointed out to the students that instead of me, LaRouche should be addressing them, but I explained, that since he was busy lecturing high level people all over the world, this wouldn't be possible, as, after all, he is but one man. So, he confines his work to where it is most effective, to seminars and conferences in Rome, India, China, Russia, the Middle East, South America, Germany, Mexico, Africa.

I suggested to the students, that ironically, LaRouche represents nothing more than a level of perception that would likely be common place throughout the world, had the post-war generations been educated according to the once thoroughly established humanist principles, rather than having been smothered with the babbling of insanity, that the countless zero-sum philosophies had served up in the imperial circuses that many of the once respected institutions have become.

I suggested therefore, that LaRouche is not fundamentally an exceptional man, but merely an Exemplar of the kind of man that everyone of humanity has the potential be with the right education, with a total dedication to the task, with an unyielding determination to succeed, and a humanity that enables one to make the sacrifices that need to be made in the struggle to advance the state of civilization.

In closing, I pointed out to the students that my lecture should now make it possible for them to seek out the kind the humanist education that makes them appreciate the substance of their humanity, and the fact that they have the potential for their glass to be filled to the brim. I suggested that this should be their guiding star, especially given the fact that humanity is fast loosing the foundation for survival of its civilization, with very few people realizing the fact, and even fewer fighting on the side of humanity. I pointed out that the student's own contributions are urgently needed in support of that fight, and that their individual contributions may make the difference between their own survival in a civilized world, and their personal destruction in a catastrophe that can still be avoided.

There was no discussion going on throughout the lecture. Consequently, I opened the floor up for questions and comments.

One of the first students who stood up asked me how I felt it was possible for a hollow generation that destroyed its industries, its financial system, and much of the world, to rebuild its economy in order to survive. The student asked how this can be done without a foundation for it, that obviously doesn't exist in a hollowed out population.

I agreed that this was a tough question to answer. I suggested that an answer has to be found, because a hollow generation is a potentially fascist generation; which is already showing through; which is evident by ever-louder cries for war, and an evermore arrogant flaunting of nuclear weapons.

That's when I remembered an article in which LaRouche had actually answered that question, by suggesting that a reverse paradigm shift is possible. I told the student about this article, and suggested that LaRouche is probably the world's foremost representative of the American intellectual tradition that the proposed paradigm shift leads back to.

I told the student that LaRouche had pointed out in this article that in the 1965 time frame a major paradigm shift occurred in America and around the world, but especially in America, which brought on a shift away from the American intellectual tradition that had been based on principles that worked; that had built a great economy and a great nation; that had successfully defeated the world's must sinister fascist empire. I pointed out that this paradigm-shift in 1965, towards America becoming fascist itself, corresponded with the time frame of the baby boomers taking over the control of the nation and much of the world, which had been brought up on an intense diet of zero-sum philosophies and ideologies. However, I also pointed out that since the baby boomers did grow up in the era prior to this shift, they had personally experienced the rich substance of the prior paradigm. In other words, they grew up in an era in which everything still worked; in which the economy functioned, which they themselves have experienced. So I pointed out to the students that the baby boomers have a foundation within their own experience to accept a return to the principles which they have experienced themselves to work, and to work well.

I suggested that the baby boomers might still be able to recall those days when they could buy a brand new car for less than three-thousand dollars, which most of them did, who then used their great dream boats to cruise down Sunset Boulevard. In fact, they could even walk down that boulevard without fear of being shot at or otherwise attacked, or being propositioned by prostitutes. They might even remember that the economy worked so well in those days that a family of four could be supported by a single worker's salary and build itself a decent house to live in. I suggested that the baby boomers could surely still remember that world that once existed, because they had been a part of that world. They saw it functioning. They experienced its dynamism. They may even remember that it was actually possible in that world for a worker to retire and live a carefree life. And as they remember all of this, which exists no more, they may also remember that a lot of the commercial enterprises of that world do no longer exist either; that the very industries that had created their prosperity, that had created their employment, even the industries that had once created their food, the family farm, are virtually gone. They may also remember that one could go to a movie in that world and not be ashamed afterwards of being a member of the human race, because of the violence that is being dished out as we have it today. They may even remember a time when they could look their friends into the eye with a smile, without this being translated into an invitation for sex as we see it so much in the world of entertainment. But mostly, when this past world is remembered, they will remember the physical prosperity they found in it, of a world in which almost everything actually worked. And if they can be induced to remember all that, they will want to get back to the world that worked, a world of actual prosperity.

Here another student stood up. He protested. "Life isn't a philosophical issue," he said acidly. "When the physical economy is gone, you can't resurrect it with philosophy."

I agreed. However, philosophy, or more correctly, the intellectual tradition behind the most advanced philosophy, is the foundation of the policies that determine how the physical economy operates, and that makes a huge difference. It determines the policies.

I told him that a long time ago a policy had been established to throw a debtor into prison, who could not repay what he owed. That policy of course made the outstanding loan even more unrepayable. The policy was so bad that it was eventually abandoned. Unfortunately, this didn't happen until it had done a lot of damage to society. Nevertheless, we still have many similar policies in force that are just as bad, which make an economic recovery virtually impossible unless some deep changes are made. This means, that quite literally, the survival of a nation, or the world, boils down to a matter of intelligent policy based on the best intellectual tradition ever developed.

I told the student who had protested, that the U.S. economy, for example is currently being strangled by thirty-two trillion dollars of debt that has been accumulated, because of bad policies. It costs the economy over seven trillion just to service that debt, which no magician in the world can squeeze out of a ten trillion dollars' gross domestic product. This means that the debt can't be repaid, especially, since even the interest can't be paid. After all, people have to have something left over to live on. So, the bottom line is, the economy is bankrupt beyond hope. But how does one deal with a totally bankrupt economy? What policies does one use?

I told the student that the present policy is to let the corporations go bankrupt when they can't pay up, even huge corporations with hundred thousand employees, and more. I told them that this sort of thing happens a lot, because the debt is killing these enterprises. I pointed out that this shutdown policy is one way in which the outstanding debt gets written off the books. I also pointed out that in the process millions of people become unemployed and destitute, and eventually many of them become homeless. And to make matters worse, which is actually the greater tragedy, the nation deprives itself of the products that these enterprises had once produced. "Now, is this a good policy?" I asked. "Is this even a sane policy?"

I pointed out that if a corporation goes bankrupt, the debts get written off. So why shouldn't one deal with the debt as a separate issue and keep the economy functioning? Why should one shut everything down?

I suggested to the students that it would have been the policy in the American intellectual tradition to keep the economy functioning, on which people's life depends, and to deal with the debt as a separate issue in a global bankruptcy reorganization. I suggested that this would be done as a matter of principle to save the economy, to save people's pensions and other essential things. This kind of action would once have been assured under the general welfare constitutional principle that was an acknowledged principle in the American intellectual tradition. But we don't do that anymore. We let everything disintegrate, which is insane. This means we have to go back to a tradition that was sane; that worked; that protected and advanced society. That is what the reverse paradigm shift is all about. That is LaRouche's policy, the policy of a man who has become an American institution, a man who fights a hopelessly seeming battle and is determined to win, because he knows that as a human being he has all the principles of the universe on his site to win this battle that he ultimately cannot loose unless the whole world disintegrates before he succeeds.

I suggested that this kind of policy fight isn't actually so much LaRouche's own personal policy fight. Rather, it is a policy fight that simply reflects the paradigms of the long established American intellectual tradition that LaRouche merely represents, a tradition that is founded in certain invariable fundamental principles that had once been acknowledged as the greatest constitutional principles in history. It is the American intellectual tradition to fight for the substance of our humanity, to develop it, and to enrich our world with it. And this is what we need to get back to all over the world, I concluded.

At this point another student stood up and gestured in protest. "I don't want to hear about your American intellectual tradition," he shouted angrily. "It's all rubbish. It's a miserable failure. America has become a failure, a sewer, its activities around the world, stink."

"That's just the point," said another student next to him in broken English, so that Wai-ye didn't have to translate, and gestured his friend to sit down.

I agreed with the student that America has become a sewer, but I pointed out that what stands behind that sewer, as the cause of it, has nothing to do with the American intellectual tradition. I told them that the paradigm shift that turned America into a sewer was the result of a crisis that was abused to destroy that tradition, and the nation with it. I pointed out that the whole tragedy resulted from a people being unable to protect themselves in a time of a deep crisis. Sure, that defense could have been accomplished were the people embracing their intellectual tradition at this critical point more fully. Unfortunately, this didn't happen. This single failure to embrace the traditional paradigm caused the tragic breakdown to occur that led to the paradigm shift that destroyed the nation. This, however does not imply that the intellectual tradition itself has been wrong, or has failed. The people had failed themselves.

I told the students what really happened. We had just come through World War Two, we had eighteen million people overseas fighting a war to restore civilization, but in the background to this war, America was being attacked covertly by the American/British imperial oligarchy that was about to be eliminated by the Roosevelt mobilized renaissance, a renaissance that was totally built on the American intellectual tradition. Then Roosevelt died suddenly. In the resulting vacuum the oligarchy saw its chance to take over the strategic area that would be vital for the nation's future, the education of its children. By the time that anyone realized what had happened, that segment of the war had already been lost.

I suggested that it is evidently easier to fight a physical war against a visible enemy, even on a global scale, than it is to fight a war against an enemy that one can't see, that works quietly in the background.

I pointed out that this singe defeat put an end to the policies of the American intellectual tradition, both in America and throughout the world. Still one can't blame the tradition for it. The tradition was extremely substantial. It had worked well. It had worked so well that a single man, as Roosevelt was, based on that tradition, could advance a nation out of its deepest economic depression to becoming the most powerful economy on the planet in just a few years, and all that while the nation had eighteen million people to support in a war overseas. This horrendous achievement all by itself, illustrates the substance of the American intellectual tradition in terms of its humanist policies, and economic policies, which are really both the same, fundamentally.

I explained that a parallel to what happened in America, could be found in the history of the Golden Renaissance in Italy, which was itself the outcome of an intellectual tradition of great substance. It started in late 1300s after the Black Death plaque had wiped out half of the population of Europe. In such a depressed situation deep questions are asked, and answered. In this case answers were found that could be traced back to the Greek Classical era, to Plato and Socrates. Out of this background a modern intellectual tradition unfolded that was established by all the great minds of the time, in which Nicolaus of Cusa played an important role. This new tradition in thinking, in humanist terms, came to life almost in the form of a universal constitution through the work done by the Council of Florence in 1439-40. This constitution established certain principles for a higher perception of man than has ever been achieved before. The intellectual tradition that stood behind this constitutional platform of a higher image of man, eventually created the Renaissance. It became a powerful renaissance force that uplifted all of Europe. When Louis XI in France built upon this intellectual tradition the word's first nation-state, the economic well being of the people of France doubled. In short, a whole new kind of nation was born.

Of course, it is no longer a secret how the Renaissance was defeated by the imperial oligarchy of Venice, how Venice introduced counteracting zero-sum philosophies; several of them, by which the Renaissance leaders were set at war against each other, that finally caused eighty years of war to erupt that quite literally drowned out the Renaissance intellectual tradition. But this demise wasn't a failure of the Renaissance intellectual tradition itself, nor did it destroy that tradition. The people had been coerced away from that tradition. I pointed out that the collapse of the Renaissance was the failure of the people to be honest with themselves, about the best tradition that has been established by the most advanced geniuses of humanity up that point.

I pointed out, that although the Renaissance was defeated, the intellectual tradition behind it was never defeated. It lived on even in the face of the imperial war philosophers like Thomas Hobbes and Hugo Grotius. Eventually, at the very depth of that war and its resulting destruction, the Renaissance intellectual tradition was rekindled and advanced further until it finally produced the world-constitutional principle that ended the 80 years of warfare that the Venetian oligarchy had set up for Europe.

I pointed out that this world-constitutional principle was established as the Treaty of Westphalia that enshrines the greatest world-constitutional principle in history, possibly even the greatest of such principles for all time to come. It has put the principle of universal love squarely on the map. All the nations of Europe signed up on it. It became a new breath for civilization. The wars were shut down. All debts were forgiven. The atrocities were forgiven. No reparations were demanded. It created a peace in Europe that lasted almost for fifty years, until Napoleon came along and rejected that principle. Then the bloody wars started all over again.

I pointed out that the Peace of Westphalia was really the result of nothing more than just another paradigm shift, perhaps the first political paradigm-shift in history. It represents a shift back to the Renaissance intellectual tradition. The USA itself, was founded on the back of this reverse paradigm shift that revived the Renaissance intellectual tradition, that set up the principle of universal love as a constitutional platform. Out of this universal intellectual tradition came eventually what is called the American intellectual tradition, since the American people's self government had become consciously founded on what has been established by the ongoing development of the Renaissance intellectual tradition.

I pointed out to the students that the so-called American intellectual tradition isn't really American per see, although it was advanced further in America. Rather, the term seems to refer to the kind of universal intellectual tradition that made America great during the few periods in which it was great. It pointed out that it is this tradition, this universal, humanist, intellectual tradition, that the whole of humanity needs to shift itself back to. I suggested that it is imminently possible that this reverse paradigm shift can be achieved again, and may be achieved when humanity finds the breathing room to do it. In 1347 society hit rock bottom. All the imperial structured had collapsed and had taken down the world around them. There was not a shred of credibility left in their claims and in their philosophies. That is when society had enough room to look at itself, and find its riches, which started the ball rolling towards the Renaissance. This happened in 1648 after half of the population in Europe had been killed in eighty years of wars. All the imperial philosophies of lies and the structures built on them were totally discredited. People suddenly found themselves with a little bit of room to look at themselves and they found in themselves something profound that they were moved to cherish and protect, and develop further.

I suggested to the students that the present world is not much better off than they were in those times of dark ages, economically and strategically. All the imperial structures are collapsing on the whole front and discredited by their massive destruction of society. Whether this gives people room again to look at themselves as in the olden days and rediscover their humanity cannot be determined. The whole world may disintegrate before this happens, at which point it will be too late. It can however be said with certainty that we have a critical choice before us to take whatever steps are needed to rediscover our humanity, its beauty, its strength, its potential, it infinite worth, and the principles that are reflected in it. Our challenge today is to put ourselves in this humanist sphere voluntarily, that until now we have only allowed ourselves to see when all the empty imperial philosophies were discredited as they collapsed our world around us. Since we would survive such a collapse in a nuclear-armed world with a globally interlinked financial system disintegrating under our feet, we have to achieve the needed transition the intelligent way. That means scrapping all the zero sum philosophies, and gaining back our humanity. That's our only chance for survival, globally.

I also pointed out to the students that the principle of the reverse paradigm shift has actually been known and understood for a very long time, since we find it illustrated as far back as in Christ Jesus' parable of the prodigal son.

I told them about the parable: In the parable a father has two sons. The younger asked the father to give him his inheritance so that he could use it and make his way in the world. But being unwise the son wasted it all, to the point that everything he had was gone. Then, at his deepest despair, when he had nothing to eat, when he was eating with swine out of the same trough, he remembered the world of his father. He recalled that even the servants lived like kings compared to him. So, he returned home asking to be made one of the servants. Well, this wish was not fulfilled. He was restored to his full honor again as a full-fledged son. I told the students that this is a beautiful example of how a reverse paradigm shift can actually begin in real life situations, like the one that we are in like now.

I pointed out that this parable represents a starting point for us to work from, since we are already worse of than the man in the story. We have hundreds of millions of people in hunger today who would gladly eat out of the trough of the swine, who are human beings nevertheless, that need to be restored to that status, to the same status that we claim for ourselves. For this to happen the whole image of humanity needs to be raised.

I pointed out that in the American intellectual tradition the nation's fundamental principles were expressed in the development of effective industries in support of our civilization that enabled people to live like human beings, with the building of infrastructures that support these industries; and with machine tool industries that build the industries that we require; industries that support farming, industries that provide transportation, industries that enable health care; with all of them supported by national banking and nationally financed infrastructure building. That is what it means to restore the human being to its rightful place and a nation to its purpose of implementing the general welfare principle and so on. There is no need for any human being anywhere on this planet to eat with the pigs, or to go hungry totally and starve to death. We have the resources within us to end these tragedies.

I pointed out that when LaRouche talks about a reverse paradigm shift back to the platform of the American intellectual tradition, he talks about a return to these constitutional principles that had become a part of that tradition by which America had prospered. He talks about them as a minimal standard for a nation and a world; a kind of threshold that one should not drop below.

I pointed out that the world was presently operating on a level that is miles below this minimal standard, which corresponds to the fact that nothing is working anymore almost anywhere in the world. Consequently, LaRouche put the Bretton Woods principle back onto the map to shut down currency speculation, as a minimal world-constitutional standard, a standard that, if implemented, will end the currency speculator's Pantheon. And since the world has become so thoroughly destroyed over the last thirty-five years, LaRouche puts forward another world-constitutional principle, which is the Eurasian Land Bridge development principle that he regards as another necessary minimal standard to create the conditions for the economic survival of humanity in a largely destroyed world. This principle, once again, is totally rooted in the various other principles established within the American intellectual tradition. The reverse paradigm shift re-establishes all those lost principles and traditions in applying these principles. There is no need to tolerate the cultivation of empty people when the future is so bright with a fully developed humanity.

The need for doing all this brings back into view Franklin Roosevelt's other world-constitutional principle, that of ending imperial rule in the world. LaRouche established on this platform a related world-constitutional principle that challenges the world's nations to establish their economies on the foundation of sovereign national banks, instead of on imperial looting institutions, and to extend to itself through these national banks low cost credits for infrastructure and industrial development, including the development of real education, humanist culture, and effective health care. It has been a long-standing element of the American intellectual tradition to keep all imperial elements out of the vital areas that are essential for the welfare of society.

I pointed out that this principle hasn't always been followed, but it had been put on the map almost from the beginning of the founding of the USA, and has now, finally, been put totally on the map by LaRouche as a minimal standard for a civilized economy. This means that we also have to go back to regulated industries in defense of the general welfare of the nation and the world, shutting down greed oriented structures, and hollow education systems.

I pointed out that all of these principles really need to become accepted world wide, as world-constitutional principles, since the world has been run into the ground and cannot rebuild itself except by a return to the minimal standards of a civilized society which these principles represent. I suggested that Franklin Delanor Roosevelt understood the need to do this when he declared that the world imperial system would come to an end. Had he not met an untimely death and served two more terms as President, imperialism would have been history and all these higher principles would have been fully established.

I pointed out that it is possible to turn the world back to that and built on it further, even to rebuild a hollowed out generation of 'empty' people and start a new renaissance. The principles for this to happen have all been laid out. All the we need to do as a society of human beings is to look at ourselves and the brightest traditions of our past to utilize the principles established there, and really do it. I suggested that this might not be an easy task, especially since hardly anybody talks about the principle of universal love anymore, and much less translates it into reality. I suggested that each individual in the world needs to become involved with that and start a reverse paradigm shift back to principle, and develop an understanding of it and apply it ones own social world together with of all the other principles.

After all this long talking I felt drained. There wasn't a thing left in me, so it seemed, that I hadn't dragged out into the open. But, apparently, it wasn't over yet. I was accused of having committed a Satanic Crime.

As we were leaving the auditorium, a group of students blocked our way. "You should be arrested," one of them said in a loud voice as he watched our reaction. "Your speech constitutes a crime against humanity."

"How so?" Steve interjected in my dense. I wasn't sure if I could handle more.

"Isn't it obvious," said the tallest of the group of four, a young man with a beautiful gentle face. He spoke is a calm manner. "You told us about Thomas Hobbes and Adam Smith, and about the empiricists and the romanticists, and you were right that their philosophies add up to zero. You told us correctly that any person educated on the basis of their philosophies ends up to be an 'empty' person because there is no constructive substance in their philosophies. You also told us correctly that the USA has two entire generations educated on this basis, which thereby have become two generations of 'empty' people. You told us that this zero-sum education now creates huge problems for America's continued existence, and more so for its future self-development. That's all correct."

41

"So what's the crime?" Steve interrupted. "What is the crime that you say we have committed?"

"Your crime is the same as the crime of Euler and Lagrange, which Gauss had proved to be a satanic crime," the tall man came back. "Except your crime is of a slightly lesser severity than the crime of Euler, who acted with the political intent to stupefy society, while you are merely guilty of the crime of omission. Still, the end result is the same, and that's tragic."

Steve just smiled. It appears there was something that he wanted to say, but evidently thought it to be wiser not to open his mouth.

"What is the crime of Euler?" our host intervened. "Be specific! If you have a charge to make, make it clear."

The man stepped forward and raised his hand, but I stopped him. "I can answer that," I said quietly. "Leonhard Euler, born in 1707, was one of the most renowned mathematicians of the 18th Century. He was the Einstein of his age. His crime was not that he put forward anything that was technically incorrect. He crime was that he gave no valid proof of the truth of what he said. The so-called prove that he put forward literally proved nothing. Euler's proof was based on imaginary numbers that he invented to make his theorem work out."

The tall young man nodded and turned to our host. "That's the crime!" he said. "Euler made his proof fit his theory, and he did it with the use of magic. He literally denied the existence of the complex domain in which the power of the human mind, the power of reason, becomes defined. Euler crossed out this entire domain. He said in essence: You have to take my solution by faith. And what choice did the people have? The people were literally forced to do that, because he gave no valid proof for what he said, and they believed him. They bowed to Euler and took his word as it were the word of God."

"The same thing is happening still," I said quietly. "Society bows to the elite and demands no proof for whatever they say. But Euler went deeper than that. His denial of proof and the imposed demand on taking everything on faith, essentially disables the scientific process of the human mind. The human intellect exists in the complex domain where we bring together what the senses tell us, with the principles that only the mind can behold. That's the domain that Euler denied. He presented a proposition and then invented magic numbers to proof the proposition, and with that he closed the complex domain. Gauss said no to that. Gauss said that all truth is knowable and provable in such a way that it becomes visually apparent that one's proposition is correct."

"I am glad that you agree, that you have committed a crime by leaving this vital aspect out of your presentation," said the tall man. "I am glad you agree that America has lost two generations that became 'empty' people not primarily because they had been taught a bunch of nonsense that adds up to zero. You seem to recognize that they have become 'empty' people primarily because their minds had been actively disabled by reductionism, a kind of thinking that disables the complex domain where the eyes and the mind come together to provide an accurate and provable view of the universe. If you disable that view, you disable what defines a human being. You reduce humanity to the status of animals. You destroy our identity, our humanity, our divine image, and our capacity to be creators to uplift and enrich the universe. That is a high crime; the highest crime that I can imagine. Euler committed this crime, and he did so intentionally on behalf of his oligarchic masters, no doubt. That makes his crime a satanic crime. And that, my friend is what destroyed two generations of human beings in the USA, in Europe, and in many other parts of the world. Not only were they not taught anything of substance, but in the process of this 'empty' teaching, their very capacity to think as a human being became actively disabled. Euler merely exemplified this crime which had countless disciples before him and after him, and with him. Humanity has since then elevated these criminals onto a high pedestal as though they were God. That is what turned two generations into 'empty' people. That is what you should have included in your lecture. That is why I am so deeply disappointed. You came so close. You began on the right note. I was overjoyed that finally somebody had the courage to expose the cause of the collapse of our civilization, but suddenly you stopped. You never addressed the core issue. I was waiting to hear you expose it. But you didn't even address it. You didn't even mention it in passing."

"Yes, that's the hidden crime that is been glossed over in the USA and in many parts of the world," said a young woman who stood next to the tall man. She spoke also in English. "It was on the basis of that that crime," she said, "that all the destructive economic and financial processes were foisted on the population, which would not have been possible without that underlying crime. Proof should have been demanded, but it wasn't. Adam Smith's disciples would have never been able to deliver this proof. A proof is not possible where there is no substance to prove. The whole destructive process would have stopped right there. But this wasn't done. Everything was taken by faith and that continues to the present day. Absolutely nobody of these entire two generations demanded a singe proof for anything. Can you imagine that? And even now, everything is taken on faith, a blind faith in the infallibility of the elite."

The tall man began to laugh. "What happened to America is so childish, one can only laugh about it. In the American environment where no proof of anything was demanded, the people found themselves being served great heap of lies. If you don't ask for proof, you expose yourself to lies. It's as simple as that. The two lost generations of America have literally become disciples of lies, and very destructive lies at that. These lies have destroyed the economies of the Americas, of Europe, of Africa, and to a large degree of those in Asia as well."

Steve agreed with the man. He turned to me. "You are guilty as charged. By not pointing out the basis for these lies," said Steve and grinned, "which would have gotten people to think from a higher level as human beings, you have been abetting these lies and their destructive effect. That is what the students accuse you of, and they are right."

"That's a crime, don't you agree?" said the tall man, looking straight at me, then at our host. Moments later he began to laugh.

"How many students do you think would have understood anything of that?" our host asked the tall man, as it were in our defense.

"That's an invalid question," the tall man replied.

Steve began to laugh. "How many of your students have studied LaRouche?" Steve asked our host. "The answer to that is your answer," said Steve. He turned to the group of four. "Obviously you have studied LaRouche's ideas."

"Of course," we have, "said the tall man and began to grin. "Hasn't everybody?" He turned to our host. "Still, I must say that your argument is invalid. Plato's Meno dialog proves that these complex concepts can be understood by anyone. When Socrates, just by asking a few questions, can get an uneducated slave boy to develop for himself the proof, beyond the shadow of a doubt, that it is possible to double a square geometrically, which involves a complex process, then anybody should be able to understand what we have just talked about, which is much less complex."

"Would you be willing to accept an assignment to teach that?" our host asked me. "As you may realize, you have the reputation already established to get their attention."

I shook my head. "That is precisely why I must decline. If I build on my reputation, then, what I would be saying? Wouldn't I likely be asking to be accepted on faith?"

I turned to the tall young man. "Why don't you teach that concept? Actually, I don't mean teaching it in the standard sense. You should illustrate the principles in such a way that your students can develop an understanding of the truth in their own mind, and thereby prove to themselves that you are telling the truth."

"You mean me?" the tall man said, surprised. "I am only a student in the school. How can I teach?"

"You are a human being," Steve replied. "And as Pete just said, you don't even want to attempt to teach. That's what the Meno dialog is all about, isn't it? Socrates emphasized that no teaching would be required to get a slave boy to start working in the complex domain, and he proved to Menon that no teaching had been involved in accomplishing what the slave boy had been asked to do. Surely, you don't suggest that your fellow students are lesser human beings than this slave boy had been?"

"I can see this to be a lot of fun," said our host to the tall young man, who was almost a foot taller than she. "If you accept the challenge you can be assured an honorable mention in the school history book, and if you do it well, you will receive a certificate of gratitude from the school."

"What about us?" the young girl who had spoken earlier, interrupted.

"Shouldn't a discussion panel have more than one person on it?" our host replied. "You are all included in the challenge."

Steve spoke up again. "LaRouche expects to have a thousand youths educated on Carl Gauss along these lines. With these one thousand youths, he will have an effective majority over the entirety of the two generations of 'empty' people, and with that he will change the course of the nation and the world. That's his plan," Steve whispered, "and he will do it."

Steve turned to the young man, and then to our host. "If you can raise the level of thinking in your school to the level that Gauss was working from - and don't make the project just a one-week affair - you can turn this school into the most powerful intellectual center of the entire region, if not of China as a whole. You will literally create geniuses here. That is the inevitable result when people begin to think and see the world in terms of universal principles. In this respect, regard today's session as but a seed crystal for the process. If you carry this through. I can guarantee you that you will develop a whole new concept of education, and you will experience it with joy."

Steve turned to your host. "Yes, you will have fun with it, all of you. As you already know, Gauss didn't dispute Euler for telling mathematical lies. Euler told no lies. He committed a more hideous crime, a satanic crime, as LaRouche says, which you said yourself is the crime of denying the complex domain in which we deliver proof to ourselves that we are human beings. Let's not commit the same crime here, and let's have fun with developing that complex domain in which we find our humanity. Gauss proved Euler wrong in his famous paper on the

Fundamental Theorem of Algebra, which simply illustrates that all algebraic facts can be proven in geometry, and thereby be demonstrated irrefutably to be correct by way of illustrating the principles involved. If that doesn't open the door to a lot of fun, what will? Gauss was no older than you are, when he did this, and he changed the world. In order to do that, Gauss had to uplift the very concept of geometry itself, out of the Euclidian space concept, to a higher level of perception of geometry. Sure, it's a hell of a challenge to get oneself up to that level. I have trouble with that myself, but it is also a lot of fun to discover how far one can go in ones understanding of the universe."

With this having been said, our host invited us and the four students to a waterfront sidewalk restaurant for tea. On the way to the Market Square, along crowded streets I had a chance to mention something to the students that they were not aware of. Actually, the students themselves prompted me on that.

"What shall we call our discussion session?" asked the young woman who spoke English well. "Shall we call it, Welcome to the 21st Century?"

Another girl, who had been silent until then, shook her head. "We should call it, Welcome to the 18th Century," she said. She spoke slowly in broken English, which was difficult for her to pronounce.

The tall man agreed. "Euler was hired to refute Leibnitz who grew up in the 'sunlight' of the Treaty of Westphalia, who through his scientific insight had become the intellectual driver behind the American independence movement. Euler tried to discredit Leibnitz, but failed, because Gauss later refuted Euler, and all that had something to do with the independence movement becoming a powerful force in the world which the oligarchy tried to prevent. The oligarchy was so scared that they staged the French Revolution in order to murder the leading edge thinkers of France, and then they created Napoleon Bonaparte a bit later, who destroyed the intellectual elite of Europe, just for that. Yes, Welcome to the 18th Century, sounds good, because Gauss fought back."

I shook my head. "If you focus on the 18th Century, you deny the achievements along this line in the 19th Century," I intervened. "At the end of the 19th Century, an American scientist by the name of Mary Baker Eddy pursued the same course as Gauss did, but within the spiritual sphere of Christianity. She had elevated the sphere of Christianity from its low Roman level, based on dogmatic religiosity that the people were forced to accept on a platform of faith. She had created a high level scientific platform for humanity, for its moral, spiritual, and scientific development. Her pedagogical infrastructures for this platform have never been surpassed, neither have they been implemented yet, except by herself."

I explained that she herself, had been highly successful in implementing that platform which is located completely in the complex domain. Through years of observation, studying, and personal experiences based on pondering the great paradoxes that Christ Jesus had laid before humanity with his profound healing work, she discovered what she called, the absolute principle of scientific mental healing. And she delivered proof, by doing her own healing work that mirrored that of Christ Jesus.

"You say that she worked her way up into the complex domain, in the spiritual sphere?" repeated the tall man. "You say that she proved this by doing the same kind of work that Christ Jesus did? You can't deliver better proof than that. But can that proof be understood? Can its geometry be understood?"

"The answer is both, yes and no," I replied cautiously. "Yes, the proof was understood, because she was able to teach other people to heal in the same manner. And no, that proof is no longer understood." I explained that she had created a vast pedagogical infrastructure that enables a student to discover in a visual manner the complex interrelationships of profound universal principles, covering everything related to being human. "It covers the whole range of human experiences, from uncovering depravity all the way up to the highest level of embracing the absolute spiritual domain. Whoever sits down and develops these pedagogical infrastructures in his or her mind will be able to determine at an instant what forces are working for or against the truth about man as a spiritual being in the image of God. All that was put in place in the latter part of the 1800s. She had used essentially the same process to refute the religiosity of Christianity, which Gauss had used to refute Euler. Unfortunately, her pedagogical infrastructures still remain largely hidden behind the cloak of secrecy. As a consequence, the science that she had discovered and founded, has been reverted back into the sphere of a religion that people take merely on a note of faith.

"So you see, Euler won again, even while he is long dead," commented the young woman who spoke fluently English. "Euler won once gain, probably for the same oligarchy that he worked for in his life, and which all the modern criminals in high places are still subservient to."

"That project of ours really gets interesting," answered the other girl who spoke English only with great difficulty.

"It gets more interesting still," I added. "The Eulers of this world may be able to hide that spiritual scientist's infrastructures, but they cannot hide the evidence of the impact of her work that had evidently been built on these infrastructures." I explained to the students that during last 35 years of that woman's life, no major victories were won by the synarchists and fascists of this world, for whom

Euler had paved the way. Her effect on the world was like that of Gauss. But that all changed soon after hear death. Within two years after her death all hell broke loose, especially in the USA. The Federal Reserve, a private central banking system, was established in the USA by an act of Congress that gave away the nation's sovereignty over its currency into private hands. This crime may yet kill us all. Also, in the same year the Income Tax system was cemented into law, and the year after that, World War I was started that the oligarchs had wanted for decades already.

The tall man, listening intently, sometimes nodded and sometimes shook his head. "That's Interesting!" he said at the end.

While we were having out tea at the sidewalk restaurant near the market square, the tall man took a napkin and drew LaRouche's triple curve on it. He pointed to it. "This is a small example of the kind of visual images that you said the woman from America had created for the spiritual domain, isn't that so?"

I agreed.

He pointed to the lower curve that he had drawn steeply declining into the negative area of the graph. "That steep decline represents the physical economy," he said. "That is what society has experienced in terms of lost productive capacity for fulfilling its needs. That decline is real. The curve represents real physical measurements of lost household income in terms of a family's available market basket. All of that has been collapsing since 1965, approximately."

Then he pointed to the steeply rising curve in the upper part of the graph. "That curve represents the rise of the values in society's financial portfolios. And what do we see if we look at both of these curves together? We see the physical production of society collapsing, and the financial values shooting sky high at the same time. In other words, these financial aggregate values don't represent anything real anymore."

"They represent a dream world," I agreed, "that is connected with the real world only in as far as the looting of the physical economy makes the financial values rise."

"Anybody who looks at these curves with an open mind will instantly recognize, beyond any doubt," said the tall man, "that this system is in a systemic collapse phase. There is no way it can continue on, and there is no way it can be saved. The graphs illustrate that reality. A single look reveals the systemic crisis that the world is in. That's the reality. A single look reveals that the world's system of greed based economics is a fraud, is doomed because of it, and can't work because it hasn't a single principle in support of it. Nor has it ever worked. The graph can be supported with real numbers. But the beauty of it is that it illustrates at a glance what forces are destroying our world. On the other hand, if you take away this simple geometric illustration of these interrelationships, and merely talk about the numbers, people can't see the principle involved and are forced to take everything on faith. In that manner society becomes exposed to also take in all the oligarchy's lies, on faith.

He sighed that the irony is, that the public is more inclined to accept the lies than to look for the truth which so easily provable. "Gauss refuted Euler, probably in order to put scientific honesty back onto the table which Euler had scrapped."

"That means nothing more, than that we have to become honest with ourselves in all areas," I said to him, "even in respect to the way in which deal with one another as human beings, including in the social domain, and this right down to the lowest grassroots level. What should motivate us there? Should we be motivated by historically trained emotions and long-standing axioms about the way things should be, that we take on faith? Or should we be motivated by recognized, universal principles that are understandable and provable?"

I pointed to the Lu Rose, our ship that was anchored nearby, that was visible from the sidewalk restaurant. Its name was clearly readable. "That's what the name means," I said. "It means that we aim to be motivated by recognized universal principles, because they are understandable and provable."

After tea, we continued our discussion on the upper deck of the Lu Rose in the light of the evening sunshine. The discussion lasted until long after the sun had set, when it was finally high time for dinner.

I wondered that night if Beethoven or Schiller had any idea as to what extent their music and their poetry might set the human intellect in motion, centuries after their death, as was happening here in that small fishing town on the far end of the world from where they stood.

The young woman, who had been our host wondered about the same thing while we were all having dinner together on the Lu Rose. "I think they knew," she said. "I think they understood their immortality. The more important question that we should ask, is this: Do we ourselves understand our immortality, or are we afraid of it like Hamlet had been, and try to shrink away from the responsibility that accepting our immortality brings with it?"

On that note the discussions on the Lu Rose adjourned that night, long after dinner, near midnight. That final question that had bee posed, remained unanswered. We all knew that this question is the very question that LaRouche had challenged humanity as a whole, to answer, and to answer it honestly. We also knew that our answer to this question would always change and would evolve and be continuously unfolding as we continue to uplift our humanity as human beings all over the world.

Part 3 - Weighing the Infinite Crime

Over dinner that night, Jacky asked me to present the same lecture at the university in Beijing.

Steve' face lit. "That's a great idea."

"It will be interesting to see what kind of reaction we get there," commented Ross.

"Sure, I present the lecture," I said to Jacky, "but shouldn't Steve rather do this, because of the language and all?"

"Why don't you both do it, together?" asked Jacky.

Steve agreed.

I told Jacky that I would like to take this one step further. I told him that I would like to offer a scholarship to three students there, of ten thousand Hong Kong dollars each, to be given to students who are best qualified to repeat our lecture in other universities, and another ten thousand on top of that, for their help in creating a video presentation that can be made available to the public television networks and to other colleges and universities.

Jacky shook his head. "I can't fund this," he said sadly, "there is no money for this kind of thing in the budget. The Universities may have some, but not that much, nor would they be willing to spend it on this."

"I will fund it myself," I said to Jacky. "There never has been any money available in the public purse for what is most essential to society. I know that. It has been like that for decades in America. It appears that your people too, have been educated by the fundi in the same manner, to disregard what is most essential for your survival as a nation. Of course, the people of the fundi don't want you to survive. They want to destroy you. Why do you think the imperials have surrounded China with a network of air bases? Still, there are a few people in the world, a precious few, who are willing to put their money on the line in order to fund these kinds of emergency projects that can really make a difference; that can wake people up!"

"Who will fund this kind of rich project for you?" Jacky remarked, and shook his head again.

"Olive will fund it," I replied. "Olive is a very dear lady, with a heart of love as wide as the world. She is a violinist with the Vienna Philharmonics. You probably have never heard of her. She works in Europe, quietly, behind the scene, but she is a real dynamo. She has done some major fund raising for me. I don't know how she did it. But she did it. The money for the project that I propose, already exists. And let me tell you, this is not a rich project, compared to what is at stake for China and its billion people. Compared to that, the cost of the project is nothing."

Steve agreed. He told Jacky a story of a small organization in Germany that all by itself, stopped a bitter war between three countries in much of the same fashion.

He asked Jacky if he could still remember the war between Serbia, Bosnia, and Croatia. He told him that this was a bitter war, that was getting worse and worse. He said to Jacky, when it seemed that the war would never end, suddenly in the midst of that utter hopelessness one of the people of this organization told him that the war would be over in a month. Steve said that he nearly ridiculed the man who told him that, so hopeless had the situation become. Steve said that he was told by his contact that this organization had intervened, and had convinced the people of Bosnia and Croatia that they were not natural enemies, but were set up against each other for somebody else's objectives. Steve told Jacky that once the people realized that, they stopped fighting each other. They banded together and defeated the Serbs who didn't want to listen to the truth, and within a single month the war was over.

"The whole project has cost less than fifty-thousand marks," said Steve, "and the money for the project was donated by a whole lot of little people, people like you and me; people who knew that this had to be done to save a nation." He told Jacky, that most people couldn't afford to make the donation for this purpose, but they did it anyway, because it was necessary, no matter how badly it hurt. "Now we need to help China in the same way," he added.

Jacky just smiled. He reached his hand out to Steve. "I'll do what I can, to help." He added that this day had become a most remarkable day.

I told Jacky that the day wasn't over yet, that we had another surprise in store for him, or rather, that Alison had. "But first I have one more surprise of my own, for you," I added. "I have nine-hundred and sixty-thousand Hong Kong dollars left in Olive's fund that I would like to use for similar kinds of scholarships in all of the major universities in China. Also, I would like to make the focus slightly different in each case; some projects focused entirely on economics, others on cultural and universal development. I also like to broaden the scope deeper into history, beyond the Renaissance, which was resulted itself from a reverse paradigm shift back to the humanist intellectual tradition of the Greek Classical era. And I want to take it back beyond that, to the very beginning of humanity's intellectual tradition. During the Renaissance period, Nicolaus of Cusa suggested that Plato and Moses have both learned some of their wisdom from Hermes Trismegistus, from the Hermetic writings, which scholars have associated with the early Egyptian God Thoth, the god of wisdom. This means that the Renaissance has its roots in Egypt and Africa."

I pointed out to Jacky that China, too has a similarly rich cultural history with an intellectual tradition that goes back seven thousand years with important cultural periods such as the Xie, the Shang, and Yin dynasties with later contributions to China's humanist intellectual tradition by the movements Confucianism and Mencianism. I told him that China has the intellectual background to stage a complete new Renaissance in the twenty-first Century, and that I wanted to help bring this about. I told him that the economic potential of such a Renaissance is likely of a magnitude beyond what anyone can imagine. It has to potential to cause a cultural uplift throughout the entire region. I suggested to Jacky, that if China were to become the intellectual center of the world, it would surely create the intellectual atmosphere in the region that will cause the natural reunification of India and Pakistan, which share a cultural history that goes back eight thousand years and includes such treasures as the Rig Veda and later the Upanishads. The division between Pakistan and India is artificial, I told Jacky. It was set up by the British Empire for the same purpose for which the animosity between Bosnia and Croatia was created, under its policy of divide and destroy, to capture the territory.

"Of course, You are invited to contribute to Olive's Humanist Development Fund," I said to Jacky. "In fact, China should make a major contribution, and it will, once people begin to recognize the economic potential that is imbedded in developing a rich humanist intellectual tradition. And for that, you might send a thank you note to Olive, for her contribution towards pulling China out of the rut."

"Pulling us out of the rut?" Jacky replied with a questioning look. "We are not in a rut."

I began to laugh. "Compared to the USA you are on an express train moving forward at high speed, but compared to your real potential, you are still in a rut," I said to him.

Tony began to laugh with me. Jacky, too.

"You seem to have no idea what a commitment to an advanced humanist intellectual tradition can accomplish," I said to Jacky. "Just look at what happened in USA. In 1929 the financial system collapsed and the great depression began.

The depression got worse and worse. People were starving. Hoover promised the people a brighter future, but he nothing to offer. He promised "a chicken in every pot." Then Roosevelt came in and everything changed. He offered a brand new world, and made good on his promise. Within a few short years the USA redeveloped itself out of its greatest depression into becoming the richest nation and the greatest economic power on the planet. And all this was accomplished while the nation had eighteen million people fighting a war overseas, which itself was a huge waste of resources. All of that was the result of Franklin Roosevelt's reverse paradigm shift back to the American intellectual tradition, the most advanced tradition in thinking that came out of Europe, that had build the USA in the first place. Can you imagine what China can do with six times the population, if this giant awakens into a Renaissance force. It will transform the world"

"No, you must be mistaken," Jacky interrupted. "It was the war buildup in the USA gave America its prosperity. Its prosperity was the result of the war, the production for the war."

"That's hogwash," Ross interjected. "That's what the oligarchy wants you believe to justify more wars. If war create economic prosperity, why isn't America booming? We have been at war with the world for decades now. We have been spending three billion dollars a month fighting wars. Why is the economy not booming? Why is it collapsing? Everything is collapsing. Even the military is collapsing logistically. We, in America, are the best example in the world to prove that wars don't create an economy, but an advanced humanist intellectual tradition does."

"I always thought World War Two build America," Jack answered quietly.

"That's a delusion," said Ross. "At the time when Franklin Roosevelt was running for election, and later became President, there was no war on the horizon. There was a war on poverty on the horizon. Poverty was deep in America in those year, but there was no world war. But Roosevelt represented the American intellectual tradition, industrialization, infrastructure building, education, a commitment to building the people up."

Ross turned to Steve, "Do you remember Roosevelt's famous four freedoms?"

He turned to Jacky again. "Those four freedoms were pretty basic really, but they gave the people a dignity that bound them together as a nation. Franklin Roosevelt's humanist principles were framed and were hung on the wall in barber shops and everywhere else, and they were fulfilled." Steve nodded. "Hitler was a nobody when Roosevelt came in, but the oligarchy was so afraid of Roosevelt," said Steve, "because of what Roosevelt represented, that they killed his counterpart in Germany and hastily financed Hitler into power. By the time the war started, years later, the USA had already recovered itself."

"We had vast infrastructure projects in progress and some completed, by the time the USA was dragged into war, reluctantly," said Ross. "By this time, the USA was already the biggest industrial power on the planet. And it was that, which saved the world from Hitler's madness. Without Roosevelt and the American intellectual tradition that he represented, Hitler would not have been defeated. But he was defeated. And he was defeated by America's logistical capability. He was defeated by the industrial machine build in America's intellectual tradition."

"The same happened during the civil war," said Steve. "The confederate South thought it would be a cake walk to take over the country, but it was to a large extend the industrial machine launched by Lincoln in the same tradition that Roosevelt used, that enabled the North to gain enough strength to defeat the oligarchic slavocray of the South. And it was much the same during the War of Independence. And in spite of all that huge waste in men and materials that went for fighting these wars, the USA prospered. That's the legacy of the American intellectual tradition, and we will see a paradigm shift back to that tradition. We will even see Roosevelt's world-constitutional principle accepted throughout the world one day soon, that the imperial oligarchy, which stood in the way of humanity and its humanist development for six hundred years, ceases to play a role."

"We will see this in our lifetime," I said to Jacky, "or we too, will cease to exist, and that's not likely to happen. History has shown that in times of every great existential crisis, a reverse paradigm shift happened that took humanity back to its highest humanist intellectual tradition. That is what we want to do now, that we want to help China to prepare itself for, in order to prevent such a crisis from happening in our time. But you must help us Jacky. You must meet us half way so that we can do this for you."

By the time our discussion came to an end it was eleven o'clock. Dagmar was putting the kettle on for tea, for a bed time snack, while Alison announced that one more ceremony needed to be performed that night, before Jacky's return to Beijing in the morning, with some of us coming along, as he had requested. She said that this was her last opportunity to give Jacky the present that she had completed only today.

Alison announced that her gift is a gift of "great value," as she had put it. She promised that its value would unfold when it is seen in the right manner, otherwise, she promised it would be of no value at all.

When everyone was assembled she brought the gift from her room, wrapped in silk paper, tied with a red ribbon. She bowed before Jacky as she presented the gift.

The gift was a portrait of Nicolai and Antonovna, reproduced from a snapshot that a guard had taken of the three of us together in the great hall of the Kremlin, on the last day that we saw each other in Moscow. Alison announced proudly that she had done the image processing herself with the equipment we had on board. The framing had been done in town.

Of course, no great speech was required to explain the significance of the portrait, since Jacky was familiar with the whole tragic story and everything connected with it.

"Obviously, the real gift is not the portrait itself," Alison added as she noticed a tear forming in Jacky's eyes. She told Jacky that she realized that our friends Nicolai and Antonovna were cruelly assassinated in a tragic escapade in which eight million other people died also, which Jacky confirmed, that he was aware of.

"I cannot mourn for the eight million," Alison said quietly, "because the scope of that is beyond my capability, but I can mourn for Nicolai. Nicolai was a man that I have come to know, and respect, and to honor, and to love. I grief for the loss of that man for the world that he had dedicated his life to, to uplift. I grief for that loss, not for my own loss, because he still lives in my heart. But mostly, I grief for his loss of life that he cherished so much. I also grief for Antonovna for the same reason, who I have never met, but have learned to love nevertheless. My heart is heavy for both of them. Greater grief than this I am not capable of. Perhaps no one is. Perhaps this is our protection, or else we die of grief. Nor is it mathematically possible for one to grief more."

She turned Jacky and asked, "What happens when one adds eight million times infinity to a single infinity?"

"The result remains infinite," he answered.

"It remains the same," Alison agreed. "The murder of a single human being is an infinite crime. That is all that I can deal with, and lament, and struggle to come to terms with. But, even as I do this, I am beginning to realize that I have added to this infinite crime."

"How do you explain this?" Jacky asked.

"The answer is not so simple, since you don't know me," Alison replied. "But ask yourself, if the murder of a single human being is an infinite crime, why are we fascinated with murder mysteries, which are stories centered on the killing of a human being?"

She told Jacky that she once had a large collection of such books. Murder mysteries, suspense novels, thrillers, entertaining books all centered on the killing of human beings. She said that she had never seen the inhumanity in allowing herself to be entertained that way. All the other kids did read those books too. They even exchanged books. She said that she actually felt sad having to leave her treasured book collection behind when we were all forced to flee the USA and the West. She told us that it wasn't until the time she searched for a photograph of Nicolai, that we could hang up in the ship to honor Nicolai's work for humanity, that she realized that she would no longer enjoy reading those books that are centered on the infinite crime.

She told us that if she had a book store she would send all those books back to the publishers, that are focused on the infinite crime, which may be ninety percent if them. Then she would search the world to find the very best the world has to offer in terms or real literature, the kind that elevates society, including the classical dramas in which the death of a human being is drawn into focus as a means for preventing the destruction of society in the real world by uplifting people to a higher level of humanity. She said that the classical drama helps, by depicting the infinite crime as an infinite crime.

Alison also said that she would do the same with videos and computer games, if she owned the relevant stores. She told us that she couldn't see herself even wanting to profit from the infinite crime. She also told us that she could never see herself to be working in the financial industry ever again, that has marginalized entire countries through looting processes, to the point that millions of people are forced into an untimely death by economic deprivation.

She told Jacky that she had made a commitment to herself, to become involved in a campaign to end this process of profiteering from, or of being entertained by, the infinite crime. She told him that this is what the portrait signified. She asked him accept it as symbol of that commitment and as an invitation to him, and the nation of China, and the world, to follow her lead.

This time it was Jacky who bowed to her, in accepting what the gift signified.

Part 4 - For the Sake of Truth.

The next morning, we were off to Beijing. A float plane took us to Poyang, connecting with the 10:30 flight to Wuhan. Four hours later we on the evening flight to Beijing, on a Boing 797 no less. Jacky's department had a place arranged for us in a government compound, something like a hotel for government business which appeared to be operated by the army. The place was clean, the service efficient, the atmosphere courteous. It was simple accommodation, but sufficient.

The official meeting started at eight in the morning.

Unlike western style business meetings, our meeting was almost a private affair. There were only a dozen people in the room, including us, that is: myself, Ross, Steve, and Ushi. To my surprise, English was an acceptable language. I should have expected this. After all, our visit to Beijing was sponsored by the economic development department that Jacky was a part of.

Once the formalities were dispensed with, a heavy set young Chinese man addressed us abruptly and asked why we were insulting China, the country that gave us refuge, by saying that China is in a rut.

"Because you are in a rut," I defended us, since I had made this statement in the first place. "You are in a rut compared to your real potential," I said to him gently. "That is the truth. The statement was not meant as an insult. In fact, we are here to help you to get out of that rut."

The fat man just laughed. "We have achieved an economic miracle during the last few decades. We have created a modern transportation system; decent housing for our people; we are self-sufficient in food production; we feed a quarter of the world's people with only eighteen percent of the world's arable land; and we have built the biggest railway network in the world for our continuing economic development. You call this being in a rut? We have even begun to build brand new cities for our people. We are not in a rut. America is in a rut."

Steve began to laugh too. "America isn't in rut," he replied. "America is dead. It stopped living thirty-five years ago. China is a dynamo compared to that. Still, China is in a rut, and is dangerously close to falling into the same trap that killed America."

Steve told the man that we were the richest and biggest economy in the world thirty-five years ago, of which there is virtually nothing left. He told him that China was drifting into the same rut that killed America. "In some respect you are already in it," he added. "You have adopted far too many of America's modern idiotic paradigms, the very same which have killed us."

The fat man shook his head. "What paradigms? What are you blabbering about? America has a robust economy. It has sky high stock market values."

"What paradigms?" I repeated. "Lots of them. Take for instance the paradigm that money is wealth. This paradigm will be killing you too, because there is no truth in it."

"You are a stupid little ex-diplomat, not an economist," said the heavy set man who appeared to be some sort of authority on economic matters. "What do you know about anything?" he added. "Money is wealth; period! Everybody knows that."

"You just proved my point," I said quietly. "The point is, that you are indeed already stuck in that rut. The wealth of society is in its productive capacity, and in the utilization of it for its self-development. That alone makes a society rich, and it has made you rich so that you can build new cities. Nothing else does make a people truly rich. Money has nothing to do with the wealth of a society. That is ancient wisdom, my friend. People found this out in the 1300s. In 1345 the entire European financial system collapsed. Puff, and it was gone. Suddenly people had nothing. Everything had been geared to money. Once this was gone, nothing worked anymore, because people thought that money is wealth, which they didn't have anymore. Consequently, nothing much was being produced anymore. The entire economy disintegrated just because the fundi's financial empire had collapsed. This collapse shouldn't have had a physical effect, but it did. The collapse had a devastating effect on the physical economy. But it wasn't the financial collapse, really, that shut the economy down. The people did that. The people themselves shut their own economy down, because they didn't see its real wealth which is in its productive capability. Had they understood this crucial point, they would have found a way to keep the economy going without the fundi's money. They could have created their own currency or devised a different system for exchanging real value for real value. As it was, they didn't do that. They shut everything down. People starved. They became biologically weak; walking shells; and when the black death plaque was brought in, it spread like wildfire and killed half the population. The devastation was so heavy in some areas that there weren't enough people left alive to bury the dead."

"What has this got to do with China?" a woman interrupted, who was sitting next to Jacky. She appeared to be his boss.

59

"The answer is: Everything!" I said quietly. "You have just demonstrated that you believe that money is wealth, like all of America does. Everybody believes that to be true, but it isn't true, as history has shown. The people in Europe believed that money is wealth, in the early 1300s. They were taught this belief by the banks. It was in the banks' interest to teach that lie to the population, because to the banks it was true. They were pirates. They stole everything from everybody. Their piracy made them wealthy, but not for long. With their privateering they destroyed the whole system. Until this last day, when the final collapse of this system happened, everything had functioned on a platform of privateering. Suddenly everything all of that became invalid. The system collapsed, because it is impossible to build an economy on the platform of stealing from one another. Unfortunately for society, most people didn't realize the truth until everything had collapsed and half the population had died."

"America fell into the same trap," said Steve. "We have become a nation of privateers. Everything we did became profit oriented, not production oriented. Everything that society required for its existence, became hijacked by the privateers and used for squeezing profits out of society. Everything that we had once built as a nation was privatized, just as the pirates had demanded, which expanded the foundation for their ever increasing looting of society. Energy production; banking; water supply; transportation; the food supply; even some highways, bridges, and the entire health-care system, all were privatized and given to pirates for privateering."

Steve laughed. "You are asking why America is dead? Just look what happened to us as a people. Our first mistake was, that we accepted the axiom that money represents wealth. With that we ruined our financial system. When the financial pirates saw their paper values collapsing, they were looking for a way to trade their paper values in for real value. Consequently, they coerced and pressured and prodded all the governments all over the world to sell their most precious national assets to the pirates. They called it privatization. This process transformed and wrecked the economies, because it changed the character of the infrastructures from being a support platform for the nations' economies, to becoming profit mill by the looting of society. It was our second mistake to allow this happen. We thereby literally gave away our privilege to love, which had once been reflected in our national infrastructure for enriching one another's existence. We gave the substance of ourselves into the hands of a 'raping' pantheon of pirates. Could any nation have dome more damage to itself than this? Hardly!"

Ross pointed out, that officially, the national assets were sold at auction, but in reality they were given away for pennies on the dollar of their real value. "They were effectively stolen from society, by the pirates, as a means for stealing more," said Ross. "Then, everyone else got into the act, too. Eventually, the entire society became profit oriented pirates, stealing from one another. The real production of things that enrich society very existence, became a secondary issue. We gave this vital task to other nations. We had to do this. Since we didn't have much of an economy anymore, we had no option but to have other nations do the producing for us, nations like China. We gave China the 'opportunity' to allow itself to be privatized, and China complied. China supplied America with industrial products which the American pirates couldn't be bothered to produce for themselves. In return the pirates gave China worthless bags of money that China couldn't use to buy much of anything with from America, since America didn't produce much of anything anymore that China could use, or very little of it. Still, China felt itself to be rich, because it was told that money is wealth. That means, that China fell into the same privatization trap as everybody else, because China, too, believed that widely accepted lunacy that money is wealth. China fell into the same trap, as America did, only in a different way, and not yet quite as deep. China's delusion that money equals wealth caused the Chinese people to willingly throw the products of their labor away, for virtually nothing in return. That means that China is literally throwing the products of its people into the garbage can, in real terms. It is trading real value for something that has intrinsically no value. That s stupid, isn't it? And China is not alone in this," Ross added. "The whole world has been drawn into this game, so don't feel badly about it."

"A society's wealth is found in the products which it is able to produce for itself to enrich its existence," I said to the lady who had asked the question in the first place. I told her that the European society figured this out in the late 1300s and created at total shift in its thinking. "Out of this shift in thinking," I said to her, "the Golden Renaissance unfolded, that became one of the greatest periods of human development of all times, and in every respect. It became one of the richest periods in history, and this without money bags standing at the center of it, or any pirates robbing society blind. These wouldn't have been tolerated. They would have been incarcerated. Of course, the people of this historic period had a little help in making this paradigm shift, because the people of ancient Greece had already laid the foundation for this revolutionary intellectual transition fifteen centuries earlier. All that the people had to do, was start the paradigm shift and to go back in time to the best intellectual tradition. They studied it, read up on it, and refined it, and of course, they took it a few steps further."

"The American people obviously can't read anymore," said Ross and laughed.

"Oh, they can read all right," Steve responded. "They read Aristotle, the traitor of humanity, who teaches them the art of privateering, who tells them that privateering is good. The whole Aristocracy is reading that nonsense, because this nonsense doesn't require them to produce anything of value. It only requires them to steal what other people produce. Stealing is easier. They even call the thieves, nobility! Stealing is noble. That is the crap that the American people read. And that is also what they are doing all over the world. They are stealing the lifeblood out of the global society, quite literally, all around the globe. And they have given themselves the laws, and the titles, and the authority, to do this global privateering legally. Nevertheless, giving the pirates fancy titles, laws, and positions of power, doesn't make their crimes against humanity right. The fact remains: Piracy can't create a productive economy, but destroys it, and thereby destroys nations. China does not stand as an exception from this."

"NO," said the fat man again, "you are wrong. How can you be babbling about piracy? America is a noble country. Maybe it is a bit ambitious, but basically it is OK."

He turned to me, as it were for a private scolding. "I am ashamed of you. I am ashamed of having you in this room. You are insulting your own country by calling America a country of privateers. The fact is, America is helping every country on the planet. Whenever a country is in trouble, the people go to the IMF and cry, bail us out, bail us out! Then the IMF goes to America, and America comes up with the money, reluctantly perhaps, but it always pays up."

Ross smiled at him. "That's a part of the problem," Ross replied. "If the American system is so wonderful, why is it, that the whole world is in trouble and keeps on running to the IMF, bail us out, bail us out? Did you ever ask yourself that question? And did you ever ask yourself why the IMF pays up, again and again?"

"The IMF has never been interested in helping a country's economic development," said Ushi, "at least not since 1965 when the IMF had been hijacked, itself. From this time onward, the IMF has become a debt collection agency for the privateers. It became a part of the restructured world-financial system, that became a system designed for privateering, that destroyed and bankrupted the world-economy. Indeed, the IMF has no choice but to pay up to bail out the bankrupt nations, because if it doesn't, its entire system becomes unglued. Not a single country that is receiving the so-called IMF bail out funds, ever sees one penny of the money anymore, it only sees its debt grow. The IMF takes all the bail-out money right back to pay for debt service demands. That's why the IMF gives it out in the first place, to avoid a sovereign default that could bring its whole house down."

Ross agreed. He said that it is utterly stupid for the nations to keep running to the IMF, asking the pirates to bail them out. "They shouldn't do it. The bottom line is, that the nations around the world are borrowing money from the IMF, some at credit card rates of interest, and this for no other purpose than to keep the IMF system alive; that is, to keep the privateering alive that is killing them economically, and is murdering their people physically in the process of it. There is nothing good in this system for any nation, for which this system deserves to be kept alive. The nations are stupid to fall for the IMF genocidal terrorist tricks."

"Actually, the nations aren't doing this voluntarily anymore," interjected Steve. "The IMF agencies and their masters whom they serve, are literally scaring the countries into compliance. They even use terrorist tactics when the mere scaring doesn't help anymore. If this happened during the Renaissance, I can assure you, the whole lot would be in jail. But nobody did this kind of privateering during the Renaissance, for the simple reason that the people didn't look for wealth in money. They found their wealth in what was being produced. But today, we live in a totally different world, with a totally different kind of thinking that border on insanity. That is why money is everything and the privateers reign supreme. Society treats them like heroes, and bows to them as they stick their knives deeper into people. On this platform the IMF has killed more human beings during its reign from 1965 on, than Adolf Hitler ever did, or ever hoped to do."

The fat man protested again. "America is a rich country," he said. "It doesn't have to resort to such tactics. And it doesn't even tolerate them. I have been there. I have seen it with my own eyes."

"You may have seen what once was, or what appears shiny on the surface, but you have not seen the real America as it exists today," said Ross. "I have lived in that country. The entire social infrastructure has been privatized, and been given to the pirates, and they are sucking the blood out of society on a massive scale."

"You should ask yourself one simple question," said Ushi. "Does a society exist to produce profits for the privateers, or does it exist to ennoble itself, to create an environment that makes living worthwhile and a rich and beautiful experience?"

"You are trying to create a renaissance!" the heavy set man interjected in an accusing tone of voice.

"Is that a crime?" Ushi asked in reply. "Naturally, that takes a bit of an effort. The environment for a renaissance must first be built. It must be created. Indeed, I agree, nobody is doing this anymore, or wants to. The whole western world has made a paradigm shift towards stealing. We have become a society of pirates and thieves. Everybody wants to profit and get rich by doing nothing. That happens on every level. And that is precisely why today's entire world-financial system is bankrupt and is falling apart, because we have shifted ourselves away from producing into stealing. Now America has come to the point where virtually nothing is being produced anymore. This means, that there is nothing left to steal, except a huge pile of debt."

The fat man just laughed. "You can't make me to believe that," he said and kept on laughing.

Ushi nudged me and handed me a small measuring tape that she had in her briefcase for some reason. It was plain to see what she was saying.

I took the measuring tape from her hand and went to the white board. They actually did have a white board in the room, with real erasable makers, not the chalk board I had expected. I measured out a square a half an inch high.

"This represents the debt load of Brazil," I said to the heavy set young man. "It amounts to a bit over half a trillion dollars. This debt load is big for Brazil. It is also big enough to bring the entire world-financial system down when Brazil defaults on this debt."

I drew a smaller square, a quarter of an inch high, a mere line really, the width of the marker. "This represents Argentina's debt," I explained. "A quarter trillion, actually less. But this tiny bit of debt is the amount that the IMF is destroying Argentina for. They are squeezing Argentina to death, because that nation can no longer pay the interest on this tiny bit of debt. People are dying, because of the IMF's insane interest collection demands."

Having said this, I took the measuring tape and measured out thirty-three inches, and drew a square of the same width, but thirty-three inches high. The white board was just large enough for me to do that. "This represents America's debt," I said to the man. I watched his face. I noticed a stunned disbelief. "Our debt is a hundred-twenty times as large as Argentina's," I said to him. "It costs us close to eight trillion a year to service that debt. But who can pay such a sum if the entire product of the entire nation amounts to no more than ten trillion a year?"

I drew an eight trillion dollar square and a ten trillion-dollar square on the board, and explained that America could service its debt alright, if nobody in the entire country required any money to eat and live, drive a car, buy closing, insurance, heat their house, and so on. I told the man, that the reason why we have this huge debt, reflects in part the fact that the economy does no longer produce enough for people to live on. "We borrow and import, and create debt. So, how do we pay the debt service charges? Well, we can't, and we don't. We roll everything over into new debt. Next year our debt will be over forty trillion. The bottom line is: The debt can never be repaid. America is bankrupt. That is why our corporations are lining up at the bankruptcy office, and a lot of pretty big ones, too. America simply doesn't have an economy anymore. There is nothing of substance left in its financial system; in its physical economy; and in its people who believe that this mess represents a healthy economy."

I sat down again and told the man that he makes the same mistake that the American people have made, who have been privatized for decades, who believe the lies that they live in a powerful and rich country, even while the economy is dead in the water and nothing is moving anymore.

The man made a gesture as if he would answer, but didn't.

"Our own people, the American people, refuse to see the reality," I said to him. "This is a disease, and the people of China have been infected, badly, with this disease. They are not as down and out yet, as the people in America, but they are suffering, and if you ask them, possibly anywhere in China, they will tell you that money equals wealth. We have a thirty-three trillion-dollar debt to prove that money does not equal wealth, that the only wealth that a society has is its productive economy of which we don't have much anymore, and the little that we have left, is privatizing society for the last drop of its blood."

"China really is in a rut," said the woman next Jacky, who appeared to be his boss. "We are trending in the same direction. O lot of things don't work anymore in our country, that used to work well. And money is always behind those failures."

"That's a dangerous position to be in," I replied. "You should realize that. You should also realize that while America is beyond being just broke, it is still a huge military power, and an insane one at that. You should also realize that this insane power is threatening China with extinction. China is surrounded by American bases. America wants to force China into a slavery position, so that it will keep America from going under, physically. That is the goal, and China lacks the military power to prevent that."

"We have spent an equivalent of twenty billion dollars annually on defense," the heavy set man interrupted.

"America spends twenty times that every year," I replied quietly, "and we have only a fifth of the size of your population. In other words, we are spending a hundred times as much on warfare preparations, per capita, than you do. We are the biggest military power on the planet. And the reason for this is rather simple. We do not only believe that money is wealth, we also believe that property is wealth, and property can be stolen. That is why we have a huge military. We want to be able to steal. We want to be able to steal the oil of the Middle East, according to our own statements, and we want to steal the oil in central Asia, and whatever other natural resources are there; just as we have declared that the resources of Africa belong to us, for which we have begun to depopulate Africa. We have said these things, and we are doing these things. Of course, it is all a sad delusion that those goals can actually be reached, because property does not equal wealth. Property means nothing in itself. If you own all the oil in the world, and you kill all the economies of the world with methods of privatization, what have you got? Nothing! Oil is only of some value as an energy resource for a thriving economy. Of course, once you realize that, you look for your wealth in the physical economy, and you channel your oil into it in such a manner as to make your physical production grow, which is your wealth. That is how the human society builds itself up, and the key element in this is not property nor money, but the human element. That is the element that drives it all; that creates the wealth; that is what needs to be enriched. And that element is something that one cannot steal with military might. This element can only be created by means of self-development."

I turned to the heavy set young man. "Yes," I said. "America is the most heavily militarized country on earth, and it is on the war path to take over the world, but it is all for nothing. There is nothing in the world that anyone can steal to enrich oneself. We either enrich one another and our world for the advancement of humanity and a richer life for all, and we do it together, or we go to hell together. Right now, the USA has chosen the going to hell option, and that should cause you to be concerned, because you are on the target list, together with everyone else."

Ross came into the act. "Our only hope is to get America, China, and the people of the world to snap out of their madness over money and stealing property, and cause a paradigm shift in thinking, back towards real economic development, the development of real wealth, all over the world. Anything less won't do. No privateering, no isolating, China is a big part of the world. It combines a quarter of the world's people. It has a responsibility to see itself in global terms as a catalyst for world development. No more silk-society kind of thinking."

"What do you mean with silk-society?" the Chinese lady asked.

"The trouble with China is," said Ross, "that is has been a silk-nation for too long. Just like the silk worms spin a cocoon around themselves, China has enclosed itself in a cocoon and pretended that the outside world doesn't exist. Thus, it feels no responsibility for uplifting humanity as a whole."

The heavy set young man stood up and pointed out that this is not really a Chinese disease. "That is a disease the whole of humanity is suffering from, especially the American society. I have travelled around," he said. "I have been in

66

your country. In your country the cocoon is so small, one needs a microscope to see it. Every family has become a cocoon, and nobody gives a damn about anybody else as if the word around them isn't a part of the planet on which they live." He began to laugh. "They don't even care for themselves. Just listen to their vocabulary. It's empty. There is nothing there. Every word is a swear word. 'Fuck you damn asshole,' someone once said to me in New York. What kind of language is this?"

I began to laugh, too. "You are right; we are the original cocooneers. But this is not an original American paradigm. That idea of a people's isolation into their own cocoons was invented in ancient times, by ancient priests, for imperial purposes. The marriage institution created those cocoons. Take one woman and one man and spin a cocoon around them. That is the game, and woe to anyone who dares to poke a hole through this web. Whenever this happened in ancient ages, it was death penalty time. Of course we don't do this anymore. Nevertheless, western paradigms are built on the same cocoonization. Hobbes affirms this. He says the principle of love doesn't apply outside of the cocoon. What is outside, isn't a part of your world. You mustn't concern yourself with it, unless you are a pirate. It's OK to be a pirate, because that isn't a part of your world. So it is OK to rape and plunder. Get a fleet of pirate ships and rob the world, provided that you are strong enough to do it. That is Hobbes speaking."

"We need a cultural paradigm shift out of this cocoonization," said the Chinese woman, the only woman in the room. "But what shall we shift back to?"

"The closest platform that we have," I said to the woman, "in terms of world-constitutional principles, that we can revert back to, are still the principles of universal love and universal sovereignty that were put on the map in 1648 with the Treaty of Westphalia. That's a challenging proposition in social terms. This challenge has never been met in all of human history. But it is possible to meet this challenge. It took us fourteen years to do this in our own little private world, but we have proven that it can be done. It was done by us on the principle of the reverse paradigm shift. The principle of the reverse shift has been used many times to rebuild the world after it had been destroyed. It was used by Roosevelt in 1932, to get America back to the American intellectual tradition. It was used by George Washington and Alexander Hamilton in 1787 to 1791, to shift America out of the mire of colonialism, back to the best European intellectual traditions that lead up to the 1648 Treaty of Westphalia. The same principle of the reverse paradigm shift was also used by the people who created this tradition. They shifted their thinking back to the best intellectual tradition established before them, that was established during the Renaissance. And the Renaissance itself, resulted from a paradigm shift back to the humanist intellectual tradition established during the Greek Classical era. If China needs help to overcome its own cocoonization, both in national terms, and in intellectual terms, we can help.

We have fourteen years of experience in exploring this reverse shift development, and how to build on this process. The question is: Do you want our help? The reality is, that you need our help in order to survive, but do you want it? That is the key question that you need to ask yourself."

We had our answer the next morning. Instead of being sent home, we were invited to four more days of meetings. The next meeting started at ten in the morning, and there were twenty people present.

"Please explain the principle of the paradigm shift in economic terms," said one of the newcomers to me. He wore a business suite, white shirt, black tie. His hair was short and neatly combed.

"Let me take you to 1932," I said to him. "America is in its deepest depression. It's election time in America. President Hoover, the depression President, is campaigning against Franklin Delanor Roosevelt. Hoover comes empty handed. Hoover inherited the conditions that caused the depression, but he had done nothing to overcome it. So he comes empty handed and promises America what must have seemed as a bunch of lies. He promised the people a chicken in every pot. To some, that lie must have sounded like a savior's call during depression times. But why was he not elected? This promise sounded hollow. No universal principle stood behind it. Thus, Roosevelt was elected. Roosevelt didn't promise the people a chicken in every pot. He promised to create a whole new world. Nor did he come empty handed with that promise. He came with George Washington in his pocket, and Alexander Hamilton, and Abraham Lincoln. In other words, he came to the election platform with America's tallest intellectual tradition in his pocket, and he promised the people, I am going to create a new world on that tried and proven foundation! And that's what the people voted for. As you know, he did deliver on his promise. When Franklin Roosevelt died, twelve years later, America had been raised out of its deepest depression to being the richest nation on the planet and the most powerful economic force that was ever created. All of that was caused by a cultural reverse paradigm shift back to the tallest intellectual tradition in existence, that had been carelessly abandoned."

"Hadn't George Washington done the same thing?" asked another man, who also wasn't there on the previous day.

"It was the same process," I agreed. "The founding fathers came with Leibnitz and Benjamin Franklin, and others in their pocket. And these stood on the achievements of all those people before them who were involved in putting the principle of universal love and universal sovereignty on the map with the Treaty of Westphalia. The founding fathers of the USA were trusted by the people, because they stood tall, not so much by their own achievements, but by the intellectual tradition they represented. They stood tall, because they stood on the shoulders of people who had achieved their own cultural reverse paradigm shift back to the Renaissance intellectual tradition, people who had Nicolaus of Cusa in their pocket. They stood on these people's shoulders. Of course, those people themselves stood tall, because they had achieved a reverse paradigm shift back across all of the dark ages to the intellectual tradition of the Greek Classical Era. That is what Cusa stood on, who came to his people with Plato and Socrates in his pocket. And when Roosevelt stood up in 1932 and promised Americans that he would create a whole new world, he stood on the shoulders of all these people rolled into one. This is the kind of reverse paradigm shift we need to create today and build on that." I pointed this out, forcefully.

At the next day's meeting we had close to fifty people in the room, with a few women among them.

"I have heard about LaRouche," one of the new people commented. "We have been told that LaRouche has been marginalized in the USA. Still, he is respected around the world. How does he fit into the patterns of paradigm shifts?"

"You can't marginalize the man," said Steve. "This can't be done. I have spoken to the man. He is one of the few rare people in our modern world who has made the reverse paradigm shift back to the tallest intellectual tradition of humanity's long cultural history. He stands tall on this collective achievement, and he comes with a lot of people in his pocket, people like Franklin Roosevelt, Abraham Lincoln, Alexander Hamilton, George Washington, Gottfried Leibnitz, Nicolaus of Cusa, and Plato and Socrates, and many others. If you want to ask: Who is LaRouche? you have to ask: Who are those people? What cultural achievement do they represent? What principles have been brought to the foreground during their life? That is why it is impossible to marginalize a man like LaRouche, who represents all of that. You can't really marginalize or slander Plato and Socrates; or marginalize and slander the Renaissance; or marginalize the principles of the Treaty of Westphalia; or marginalize the founding principles of the United States of America; or marginalize its profound intellectual tradition. You can close your eyes to it, but you can't marginalize that history, or slander that history. It remains as valid as it was on the day it was made. It is a fact of history that America rose from its worst depression to become the greatest industrial power on the planet in less than a dozen years. You can't marginalize that, or slander that achievement. This happened. This is the manifestation of America's intellectual tradition. This is what LaRouche brings to the table, with both pockets filled to the brim. You can't marginalize a man like that. You can deny the man, but this means denying your own cultural substance. Sure, you can spout out slanders, but in doing so you would only slander yourself by

69

demonstration to the world that you haven't got the faintest idea of what you are talking about."

"That's not what I wanted to hear," answered the woman. "Can you give us some examples of policy?"

"I can do this," Ushi answered the woman. "We all knew what Roosevelt did. That describes LaRouche's policies. But that is not what you want to hear, either. So, let's take a look at a single policy, the return to regulated industries, for instance. The principle had been established during the Renaissance that money is not wealth. It had been established that all the wealth of society is derived from its productive activities. For this industry to function, that is, what makes our human productivity efficient, we need to create infrastructures, such as electric energy systems. So, how do we create efficient energy systems? If we were to say: Well, we need them, so let's get the state to build them for us, we would fulfill the principle of universal love that is reflected in the general welfare principle of the constitution. But does this accord with the highest principle discovered in mankind's long intellectual development? It does not. The principle of universal sovereignty is not represented. This means that we have to invite all the entrepreneurs to get themselves into the act of creating electricity for society. If we were to do that, of course, we would throw the field wide open to the scourge of pirateering, which shuts down the very idea of economic development. So, what do we do? We take the principle of universal love, the general welfare principle, and combine it with the principle of universal sovereignty. This means that we say to the entrepreneurs: the field is wide open, hop to it and generate electricity for the betterment of the nation; but you have to do it within the boundaries of a regulatory system that assures that the development of the nation is well served. This dual focus on universal sovereignty and universal love, as it were a single principle, closes the door to pirateering, and opens it to effective competition to create the best energy systems and other industrial infrastructures that society can provide for itself. That is what stands behind the policy for industry regulation. It is a simple policy, but it is deeply rooted in the brightest discoveries of humanist intellectual traditions. This, for example, is one of LaRouche's policy platforms."

I added that this principle of drawing together the two principles of universal love and universal sovereignty, in such a way that the two principles define one another, actually became the foundation for the 1648 Peace of Westphalia. "It became the principle of civilization," I said forcefully, emphasizing this point. "Universal sovereignty became redefined. It became uplifted from being the universal right of might, to being the guarantor for the universal rights of man. And by the same token the principle of universal love was redefined and uplifted from being a universal duty, to being a universal privilege, a privilege that is inherent to being human."

I pointed out that LaRouche represents this platform to the fullest extend anyone is in our modern world, and that he had begun his fight to re-establish this platform ever since it had been set aside in 1965 for the privileges of the new Pantheon.

I suppose, we must have impressed them, because they allowed us to continue.

On the fourth day the discussion was centered on why China should support LaRouche.

This time the meeting was held in the auditorium of the government building. The auditorium wasn't full by any means, but there were at least a hundred people in attendance. The moderator of the panel, a man with a stern expression, but with a kind tone of voice, asked me to deliver the keynote speech, and then he introduced me personally.

He made a fine introduction. Also, it was he who chose the theme: Why should China support LaRouche?

Wow! Suddenly, there I stood, a hundred faces staring at me, and I was demanded to deliver. That's when I remembered Franklin Roosevelt, who had brought to the table the entire American intellectual tradition, and he won the hearts of the people with his offer to create a new world. I realized at this moment that I had more in my pocket than he did, and this, I realized, was something that I could easily talk about all day long.

I also remembered Olive's story. I told the people in attendance in the auditorium the story that Olive had told me at our last meeting on the West Coast of Vancouver Island, at a tiny resort at Point No Point. I suggested to the people that China is in the same position than the people are who are described in that story, together with everyone else around the world. I reminded them that the USA was about to launch a global war on civilization in a hopeless quest to create a world empire. I pointed out that the quest was hopeless for the USA, since such an empire can never be build, and it was hopeless for humanity too, since any attempt to build this kind of empire would destroy the world, including the USA and China, especially China.

I told them that China is the number one target in America's quest for world domination, because it poses the greatest threat to its would be empire. This threat lies not in China's military might, I assured them, which is minuscule, but lies in China's potential for economic development. I pointed out that for this reason, China and all of Asia is scheduled to become transformed into another Africa, a minutely subdivided, impoverished, war-torn, dying continent. That is what is at stake.

I told the people that the only course of action that can save China, is to create a deep reaching cultural paradigm shift throughout China, unfolding on every level, down to the grass roots level, that links society back in time to the principles established during mankind's brightest periods, based on the tallest intellectual traditions that were created during the last twenty-five hundred years of mankind's humanist and scientific development. "That is what LaRouche represents," I said to them, "and that is what everybody else around the world must also represent. Since this kind of a goal is not easily won, LaRouche must be seen in the minds of the people all over the world as a resource for their own fight, a kind of political resource that has the potential to alter the policies of the government in the USA and in other nations."

I pointed out that if the people around the world don't see LaRouche as a resource, they are not in the fight to save their civilization, and consequently, civilization will collapse. I told them that Russia tried this once in terms of their antimissile defense, and destroyed themselves economically under the resulting burden, as LaRouche had warned them say would. I suggested that the same can happen politically. Standing isolated by itself, China will likely be torn apart as planned. In the process, huge numbers of the world's people will die.

I told them that this is the reason why LaRouche is a valuable resource for them in their own, and absolutely necessary, fight to save their world. I told them that without this resource, they have no hope. Since America owns the military machine that can carry out the destruction of the world, the fight for a policy change had top begin within the United States itself. This is what LaRouche aims to address. I told them that this makes his fight, their own personal fight, even the fight of every human being on the planet, because there exists no one on this planet who is not affected by the outcome of this fight. This means that LaRouche must receive the kind of support from around the world that is required to put him into a position to reorganize U.S. policy away from the war policy, to a renaissance policy. If it is necessary for him to be in the White House to do that, then the whole world must organize itself in such a manner that its actions will put him there, because it is in their most vital interest. And why shouldn't it be possible to do this? I pointed out that LaRouche stands on a taller platform than the one that Franklin Roosevelt stood on when he promised the American people a brand new world, who was then given the chance to deliver. The outcome from

72

that election changed the world. It literally saved civilization. Had Hoover been elected, Hitler would surely not have been defeated, and might have ruled the world in awesome murdering way.

I pointed out that LaRouche stands not only on the platform of America's tallest intellectual tradition, as did Franklin Roosevelt, but stands on the entire platform of the tallest intellectual achievements in human history, especially those of the last twenty-five-hundred years. There exists no other leader on the American political scene today, or on the global scene, who can say that, or who comes even close to be able to say that.

Certainly, I agreed, that there is a need for China and other nations to develop that kind of leadership for their own self-government, but I pointed out that in today's time of intense crisis, everything must be focused onto the already existing potentials to carry forward the fight, and to carry it forward at the critical world-strategic flash point inside the USA, where the battle will be decided, and where LaRouche is fighting at the leading edge. No military commander would ever pull troops away from the most critical strategic battle in a war. To the contrary, he would throw every available resource into this battle, for if this battle isn't won, nothing matters afterwards. This must be the attitude of every human being towards LaRouche, and that of every government and nation towards him, because LaRouche must be seen as a vital focal point of their own fight for survival.

I pointed out that LaRouche doesn't exist outside of our universal family, called humanity. He is a part of our humanity. His fight is our fight for the principles of universal love and universal sovereignty as a single principle, the principle of civilization. We have the privilege to unite with that man, and not just to save our own skin, but to re-establish the principle of civilization for our posterity and to advance its cause for the benefit of all future generations. This the privilege of love in the highest sense, in which we find ourselves to be truly human.

"And still, we must take the LaRouche issue one step further," I said to the audience. I pointed out that LaRouche is over eighty years old: he may die soon; indeed, he will die in the due course of a human being. "But will this eventuality end the necessary fight for civilization?" I asked. "The principles that he stands for are universal principles. They are our principles. The foundation for the Peace of Westphalia is also our foundation. The unity of the principles of universal love and universal sovereignty must live in us, because it is the foundation for our civilization. It must live in all of us and be supreme, because the human being is the supreme being in this universe of ours."

I pointed out that when Franklin Roosevelt called the world-leaders together to establish the Bretton Woods post-war monetary system on the principles of civilization, he acted with the authority of the supreme commander of the greatest military and economic power on earth. I suggested that we can go beyond that, that we can make the same call for action by a still higher authority, our authority, the authority of the human being as the supreme being in the universe. "We are supreme," I said to the people, "because the principles of our humanity, the principles of universal love and universal sovereignty drawn together into the principle of civilization, makes us supreme; it uplifts us beyond ourselves, even to the privilege of a love for one another, for ourselves, and for our posterity, in which we find ourselves to be fully human. On this platform, we are supreme. Without it, we amount to nothing. Without it we'll end up as dead as the American economy already is, as western society largely is. The LaRouche process has to be carried forward within us on the platform of our privilege as human beings to live and love, to develop our humanity, to build, create, discover, care, honor, uplift and enrich one another, and to find our happiness in the dimension of being alive on that platform as a human being."

As some applause developed, I raised my hand to stop it. I wasn't finished. "We must go further than this," I pointed out. "We must recognize LaRouche's leadership in this fight, which is also our own individual fight. Therefore, we need to ask ourselves: What is real leadership?"

I pointed out that some people are taught to equate leadership with dictatorship, and for good reasons, because most people simply don't know what real leadership is. "Yes, there are many people at leadership positions who are dictators," I said. "These are people with a strong will. Often they are people with little humanity in them, who represent ideologies that push society over the edge. They are usually people who bedazzle society with meaningless speeches, empty promises, and irrational ideals; who lead society into great crises of economic collapse, even war. But this bedazzlement, the kind that can be measured in popularity polls, is not a measure of leadership. Leadership lies elsewhere."

I pointed out that real leadership is defined by its effect on the development of civilization. I gave an example. "Let's look at the earliest stage of civilization," I suggested. "The first person who utilized the best established intellectual tradition, however faint that might have been at the at the early stages of civilization, discovered and utilized the principle of agriculture, for instance. The person who did this was a real leader. That person utilized the most advanced tradition of thinking that had been developed up to that point, and uplifted society with it to a higher level of physical existence. That person literally created a revolution in living, an uplifted form of civilization. That is how leadership can be measured."

74

I suggested that this person didn't likely force the others what to do, like a dictator would. Nor would this person likely have been recognized as a leader, who merely illustrated the utility of a beneficial principle that other people were able to understand and use to create a better world for themselves.

I pointed out that the same attributes still define leadership in today's world. "Today's leader is a person who represents the best of mankind's intellectual tradition, developed through the ages," I said this firmly, to emphasize this fundamental fact. "A real leader represents the principles that have been developed in that tradition, that have historically elevated civilization. A leader is one who is able to draw together all the developed traditions and principles, and is able to apply them to current situations in order to elevate society anew, back to the highest previously established humanist platform, and then a step further. Such a leader will never be a person who tells a people what to think. Instead, the leader will support society's own self-development as a human being. That support will be drawn out of the depth of the leader's advanced self-development that defines the leadership qualities. A leader, therefore, is a person who is sufficiently ahead of society's self-development to be able to make the leading principles of mankind's history accessible to society; who can warn of subtle errors; who can encourage the budding consciousness to reach ahead; who can also give a credible assurance by example that a person is able to reach incredible heights of scientific perception and effectiveness as a human being."

I pointed out further that a real leader is also a profoundly human person, a person who can inspire society to respond to tragedies in such a way that the suffering that has been incurred will not have been suffered in vain, but can be used as a catalyst to raise the platform of thinking above the failures that caused the tragedies, in order to create a world in which such tragedies cannot occur again. "A true leader," I said to the audience, "will not respond to war atrocities with cries for retribution, as one hears this so often, but will respond with policies for elevating all parties in a way that can serve as a platform for winning the peace."

I pointed out that LaRouche is a leader in terms of all of these definitions, because he has that kind of an effect on society's self-awakening. I also pointed out that all of the massive slander that is routinely directed against such leadership, always comes to light in the end as an indictment of the slanderers themselves, because a true leader represents the truth, and one cannot slander the truth without advertising one's own ignorance of it. I also pointed out that the same holds true in the positive direction. Whoever supports a great leader with his or her own understanding of the truth, will invariably be recognized by those who seek the truth, as a person with leadership qualities of his own. I suggested to the people in the audience that this attribute applies to countries as well as to individuals. I pointed out in this context that China is a nation with a profound cultural tradition, and has therefore a well established background to put itself into this kind of leadership role, and that this role invariably also involves supporting the most advanced individual leaders in the world. I suggested that it is in China best interest to develop this kind of national leadership position, centered on LaRouche's leadership, as some other nations were already in the process of doing.

I suggested that once this larger threshold towards the truth is being crossed around the world, the terrible dangers that exist in our world, will surely end. "If this happens," I said firmly, "we will win the fight that we must win for our civilization to survive; and we will see in our lifetime the beginning for a new world without poverty, persecution, and war."

To judge by the people's applause, I felt that I had made a successful speech that day. But would anyone remember a word of it the next day? Would everything continue to be business as usual?

I remembered Fred's comment after the Caracas conference was over, were countless great speeches had been made, while few actions resulted from them. Fred had been right in his comment. His comment had been, "and so, the world grinds on."

As I left the conference hall that day, I was filled with a buoyant hope that the response would be different this time. It was encouraging to note that during the course of my speech and the long discussion that followed, the audience had increased in numbers to almost five hundred. Maybe the world would not just "grind on" this time around. Maybe a reverse paradigm shift had really begun to unfold.

Editorial: Fighting for the Truth

By Rolf A. F. Witzsche - 12/3/2016

The ancient scourge of ecclesiastical despotism, rather than having been healed, has been allowed to expand into the domains of science, civilization, politics, and economics. The world is in a rut. Who speaks for the truth?

Oh yes, the world is in a rut indeed on all of these fronts. Physical Science, for example, has been choked to death with the scam-doctrine of manmade global warming, or manmade climate change as it is now called, which has not one aspect of truth in it, for which upwards to 100 million people are murdered each year with starvation under the biofuels hoax. Vast amounts of agricultural resources are diverted to be burned as motor fuels for no benefits whatsoever. It takes huge areas of lands to grow the crops that become fomented into roughly 600 billion gallons of alcohol hooch, that becomes distilled to over 90 billion gallons of 99% pure alcohol, termed ethanol that is added to gasoline and burned with it, at 65% lower energy output. Nor is it pollution free. The mass-burning of this alcohol-type fuel produces a number of carsogenic air-pollutants. It is a neurotoxic, psychoactive drug. When it is burned, it produces atmospheric formaldehyde, acetaldehyde, carbon monoxide, nitrous oxides, ozone, and nearly doubles the carbon dioxide emissions when one counts the emissions from the burning of carbon fuels that are required to produce the ethanol. Almost as much energy input is required to produce the ethanol fuel than the fuel gives back. All considered, the biofuels process is a highly expensive and inefficient energy conversion process, rather than being a net energy producer. It is highly efficient, only in murdering people. The volume of agricultural resources that are diverted to be burned, would normally nourish 400 million people. In a world that has a billion people living in chronic starvation, the mass-burning of food is murdering most likely 100 million people a year, for no benefit whatsoever, with vast segments of society participating in the holocaust at the gas pump. That's the face of science despotism, which society obediently bows to. Political objectives now determine with known lies, what is scientific truth. And this is only one single aspect on a wide horizon of similar aspects, and the smallest of them in terms of consequences.

Science-despotism, if it is not reversed soon, may ultimately destroy civilization and 99% of humanity with it. The day of this happening is not far distant. A large volume of physical evidence exists that a phase shift in the solar process will likely occur in the 2050s timeframe, which will diminish the Sun's surface temperature from the present 5,800 degrees (Kelvin) to roughly 4,000 degrees, for a 75% reduced solar energy output; with which the next glaciation cycle begins, commonly termed the Ice Age. The weakening of the solar system towards the phase shift is already in progress. The evidence is so numerous that nearly two dozen video presentations were required to present it. The presentations can be found on my website under the heading, "Cool Science for Kids to have a future in an Ice Age World." See: http://www.ice-age-ahead-iaa.ca/000/index.html

The Ice Age transition itself, promises to be a quick one, in the range of days and weeks, not the thousands of years that mainstream science is preaching. The time we have left to get ready is short, indeed, and the task is enormous, though not impossible.

To get ready, we need to built 6,000 brand new cities from scratch and have them completed and occupied in roughly 30 years. The new cities are required to enable the relocation of all the nations that a presently located outside the tropics, into the tropics, together with their agriculture, their industries, and cultural institutions. Since there is little suitable land in the tropics, the new facilities and infrastructures will have to be placed afloat across the equatorial seas.

To fail on this front amounts to committing mass-suicide. Researchers tell us that only 1-10 million people had made it through the last glaciation period alive. This is roughly what the primitive Earth can support by itself in an Ice Age world, without technological infrastructures. Without truth in science, and following that, truth in politics, culture, and economics, we are lost. Lost here means, to be people without a future.

The entire novel that these 4 parts are elements of, named Lu Mountain, which is the last of a sequence of 12 novels, is focused on the question, 'where do we go from here?' This asks, what progress must we make to have a future?

The obvious answer is that the train to the future must stop at many stations along the way. The 4 parts presented here are stations far down on the track. The first station needs to be named: Despotism Ends Here.

The break with despotism is what the story of the posters with dragons is focused on. If we cannot get to this 'station' on the track, the land beyond cannot be reached. This is what the CSD concept signifies. It was developed in the early years of the 1900s by a New England woman, named Mary Baker Eddy. She was one of the great pioneers of her time.

She had suffered a severe spinal injury in 1866, that was said to become fatal. While near death, she found herself suddenly healed, by some evidently profound spiritual reasoning. She set out to discover the science of what had made this healing possible, and in the course of it, began to teach others to heal on a scientific spiritual basis. She founded a college for this purpose, in 1883, that became known as the Massachusetts Metaphysical College. In the mean time she founded a church to perpetuate and expand her science, which she named

Christian Science. As this task required all her time, she closed the college in 1889, in which she had personally taught over 4,000 students. She stopped teaching, but retained the charter for her college, and her position as its president. She reopened it 10 years later as an auxiliary to her Church in a symbolic manner, by making no provisions for teachers that would teach in the college. Instead, she set up a Board of Education that would carry on some basic teaching, but was only allowed to issue the bachelor's degree CSB. She awarded the higher degree, CSD, to those who were taught by herself personally. Here comes the crux of the matter that remained almost hidden. In the appendix to her Church Manual, she provided sample application forms that stipulated that the membership application needs the countersigner to be a person who has passed examination by the Board of Education, or one who has taken a degree at the Massachusetts Metaphysical College. With the college having no teachers provided for it, the process of taking a degree at the college remains only possible symbolically, and is only possible to be certified by the accomplishments achieved. It is as if she was saying to society that at the leading edge one is alone. No one is qualified there to stand as judge over another, render examination, and award certificates. In this case the pioneer closed the door to ecclesiastical despotism, if only in principle.

This pioneering example is important, because in our modern time science has become choked with certified despotism. The entire manmade global warming doctrine rides on the elitism of certified despotism. Truth no longer has a voice. This also means that society no longer owns its own thinking. Truth becomes politically determined and despotically imposed. It is almost impossible in modern time for society to get itself off the Global Warming Train to hell that runs in the opposite direction, away from the future, hiding the real nature of the Ice Age dynamics in order that humanity will not create itself a future, but lay itself down to die, instead. The science despotism serves the dream of mass-depopulation to preserve a feudal system of empire that has no place left in the world to actually exist. As a looting system, it has destroyed what it is feeding on.

The challenge to overcome despotism is evidently one of the greatest challenges in modern time. Mainstream astrophysics has become a club of certified liars, like a number of other departments of science from politics to economics to environmentalism.

Without the despotism that chokes the world, the needed 6,000 new cities would likely be built with ease, which seems presently impossible, and definitely so under the tragically still-prevailing western financial doctrine of private imperial monetarism. The tragedy that maintains the despotism that chokes the world, especially the western world, is the disease in civilization, called elitism. Elitism and despotism are one, and this one renders humanity so small, mentally, that society now argues against its very survival. If the 6,000 new cities are not built, that enable the relocation of the nations outside the tropics, into the tropics, civilization will end when the solar system's Ice Age phase shift occurs. The despotism of elitism almost assures this. It assures this with the same certainty as the military nuclear-war-posture doctrine of Mutually Assured Destruction, ultimately assures the destruction of the world and nearly all of humanity with it. The disease of elitism in civilization, which keeps the mind small, boxed in, and artificially confined with politically motivated lies against man, will murder humanity collectively with near-perfect assurance if the disease is not healed. It is a fatal disease. It has always been that. It is a disease that demolishes the truth in the sight of man as if it didn't exist. The disease renders everything mortal, even humanity itself. It preserves nothing. It diminishes everything, by which the most precious crumbles into dust.

The story in this book has 4 parts. The first part is focused on reaching for the pinnacle of what is good and beautiful in humanity, which is the foundation for civilization.

The second part is focused on the rights of humanity to know the truth about itself, and its freedom rooted in the truth.

The third part is focused on understanding and on acknowledging in a scientific manner the power that each one of us has as a divine human being, to uplift the world, in which the value of the human being comes to light.

The fourth part is focused on the renaissance potential that is inherent in a spiritually uplifted self-perception in society. That's what economics is all about, isn't it? Economics is built on a spiritual foundation, of Love expressed as love, meeting the human need as efficiently and as fully as possible. Economics is a process of uplifting physics into the realm of metaphysics. The whole of society presently lives by man-created resources that are enabled by scientific and technological processes, which far supersede in their creative and productive capacity what the natural world, on its primitive platform, is able to provide.

Further references for this type of 4-part progression can be found in my book, *Christian Science and Christ and Christmas*. *(see: http://www.ice-age-ahead-iaa.ca/christian_science/Christian_Science_and_Christ_and_Christmas.html)*

As a highly developed spiritual humanity, we have achieved wonders on this path of scientific and spiritual development, though we have barely begun to develop this potential. In spite of the grand achievements that have been wrought from time to time throughout history, the Ice Age Challenge before us puts all of these achievements into the category of a mere beginning. I say this in comparison with the creative and productive power that is inherent in our humanity as human beings, and as the greatest gems on the planet.

The potential still exists at the present time to meet the Ice Age Challenge and to assure one-another a bright and richly livable future. However, if we continue to bow to the despotism of elitism that chokes humanity as the terribly dangerous cultural disease that it is, we will remain stuck in the easy chair under the thumb of despotism, and do nothing towards having the grand human future that we are capable of creating. In this case we cannot escape the consequences that promise to be infinitely worse than the horrors of the world wars in which society has destroyed continents and nations as a 'little' people from the throne of self-denial at the bidding of its despotic elite. We can stop this train of history and reverse direction. Russia and China have already begun this reversal, and made a significant starting contribution in a number of grand respects with their commitment to war avoidance and world development. Whether this is enough, and unfolds fast enough to inspire the world to comply with the astrophysical Ice Age Schedule, remains to be seen. The world is in the twilight in this respect. Nevertheless, in considering the speed with which the turn-around is already unfolding, inspires justified confidence that the vastly greater Ice Age Challenge will yet be met.